Say It Right in

SPANISH

Second Edition

Easily Pronounced Language Systems

Clyde Peters, Author

New York   Chicago   San Francisco   Lisbon   London   Madrid   Mexico City
Milan   New Delhi   San Juan   Seoul   Singapore   Sydney   Toronto

1 2 3 4 5 6 7 8 9 10 11 12 13 14 15   QFR/QFR   1 9 8 7 6 5 4 3 2 1

ISBN   978-0-07-176691-3
MHID   0-07-176691-X

Library of Congress Cataloging-in-Publication Data

Say it right in Spanish / Easily Pronounced Language Systems — 2nd ed.
       p.   cm. — (Say it right)
   Includes index.
   Text in English and Spanish.
   ISBN 978-0-07-176691-3 (alk. paper)
   1. Spanish language—Pronunciation by foreign speakers.   2. Spanish language—Spoken Spanish.   3. Spanish language—Conversation and phrase books—English.   I. Easily Pronounced Language Systems.   II. Clyde E. Peters, Author.

PC4137.S28   2011
468.3'421—dc22   2011011058

Clyde Peters, author
Luc Nisset, illustrations
Betty Chapman, EPLS contributor, www.isayitright.com
Priscilla Leal Bailey, senior series editor
Francisco J. Madrigal, Spanish language consultant

Also available:
Say It Right in Chinese, Second Edition
Say It Right in French, Second Edition
Say It Right in Italian, Second Edition

For more titles and apps, see page 179.

Perfect your pronunciation by listening to sample phrases from this book. Go to www.audiostudyplayer.com, launch the Study Player, and then select: Spanish>For Travel>Say It Right in Spanish.

McGraw-Hill books are available at special quantity discounts to use as premiums and sales promotions or for use in corporate training programs. To contact a representative, please e-mail us at bulksales@mcgraw-hill.com.

This book is printed on acid-free paper.

CONTENTS

INTRODUCTION

The SAY IT RIGHT FOREIGN LANGUAGE PHRASE BOOK SERIES has been developed with the conviction that learning to speak a foreign language should be fun and easy!

All SAY IT RIGHT phrase books feature the EPLS Vowel Symbol System, a revolutionary phonetic system that stresses consistency, clarity, and above all, simplicity!

Since this unique phonetic system is used in all SAY IT RIGHT phrase books, you only have to learn the VOWEL SYMBOL SYSTEM ONCE!

The SAY IT RIGHT series uses the easiest phrases possible for English speakers to pronounce and is designed to reflect how foreign languages are used by native speakers.

You will be amazed at how confidence in your pronunciation leads to an eagerness to talk to other people in their own language.

Whether you want to learn a new language for travel, education, business, study, or personal enrichment, SAY IT RIGHT phrase books offer a simple and effective method of pronunciation and communication.

PRONUNCIATION GUIDE

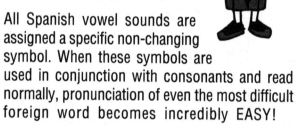

Most English speakers are familiar with the Spanish word **Taco**. This is how the correct pronunciation is represented in the EPLS Vowel Symbol System.

All Spanish vowel sounds are assigned a specific non-changing symbol. When these symbols are used in conjunction with consonants and read normally, pronunciation of even the most difficult foreign word becomes incredibly EASY!

On the following page are all the EPLS Vowel Symbols used in this book. They are EASY to LEARN since their sounds are familiar. Beneath each symbol are three English words which contain the sound of the symbol.

Practice pronouncing the words under each symbol until you mentally associate the correct vowel sound with the correct symbol. Most symbols are pronounced the way they look!

THE SAME BASIC SYMBOLS ARE USED IN ALL SAY IT RIGHT PHRASE BOOKS!

EPLS VOWEL SYMBOL SYSTEM

(A)

Ace
Bake
Safe

(EE)

See
Feet
Meet

(I)

Ice
Kite
Pie

(O)

Oak
Cold
Sold

(OO)

Cool
Pool
Too

(ĕ)

Men
Red
Bed

(ah)

Calm
Mom
Hot

(oy)

Toy
Boy
Joy

(ow)

Cow
How
Now

EPLS CONSONANTS

Consonants are letters like **T**, **D**, and **K**. They are easy to recognize and their pronunciation seldom changes. The following EPLS pronunciation guide letters represent some unique Spanish consonant sounds.

Ŗ   Represents a rolled **r** sound.

Ŗ̰   Represents a strongly rolled **r** sound.

V   Represents the Spanish letter **v** and is pronounced like the **v** in **v**ine but very softly. Depending on your location you will often hear the Spanish **v** pronounced like the **b** in **b**oy.

B   Represents the Spanish letter **b** and sounds like the **b** in **b**oy. Sometimes, the Spanish **b** is pronounced so softly that the lips barely touch.

D   Represents the Spanish letter **d** and sounds like the **d** in **d**ay. Sometimes, the Spanish **d** is pronounced softly and sounds like **th** in the English words **th**ey or **th**en.

T̲H̲   These EPLS letters are underlined to remind you that the letters are voiced and sound like the **th** in the words e**th**ernet or **th**ink. You will find this pronunciation common in Spain.

PRONUNCIATION TIPS

- Each pronunciation guide word is broken into syllables. Read each word slowly, one syllable at a time, increasing speed as you become more familiar with the system.

- In Spanish it is important to emphasize certain syllables. This mark (´) over the syllable reminds you to stress that syllable.

- It is estimated that nearly 300 million people now speak Spanish around the world. Don't be surprised to hear variations in the meanings and pronunciation of some Spanish words. **To perfect your Spanish accent you must listen closely to Spanish speakers and adjust your speech accordingly.**

- The pronunciation and word choices in this book were chosen for their simplicity and effectiveness.

- In northern Spain, **z** before any letter and **c** before **e** or **i** are pronounced like the **th** in **th**ink. In southern Spain and most of Latin America, **z** by itself and **c** before **e** or **i** sound like an **s**. In this phrase book the **s** sound is used for **z** and **c** because of its wider usage throughout the Spanish-speaking world.

- **PFV** is an abbreviation for **por favor** which means "please" in Spanish. You will see it used throughout the book.

ICONS USED IN THIS BOOK

 ## KEY WORDS

You will find this icon at the beginning of chapters indicating key words relating to chapter content. These are important words to become familiar with.

 ## PHRASEMAKER

The Phrasemaker icon provides the traveler with a choice of phrases that allows the user to make his or her own sentences.

Say It
Right in
SPANISH

ESSENTIAL WORDS AND PHRASES

Here are some basic words and phrases that will help you express your needs and feelings in **Spanish**.

Hello

Hola

 O-La

How are you?

¿Cómo está?

KO-MO eS-Tah

Fine / Very well

Muy bien

MWee Bee-eN

And you?

¿Y usted?

ee ooS-TeD

Good-bye.

Adiós

ah-Dee-OS

Good morning

Buenos días

BWĔ-NOS DĒ-ahS

Good evening / Good afternoon

Buenas tardes

BWĔ-NahS TahR-DĒS

Good night

Buenas noches

BWĔ-NahS NO-CHĔS

Mr.

Señor

SĔN-YOR

Mrs.

Señora

SĔN-YO-Rah

Miss

Señorita

SĔN-YO-RĒ-Tah

Yes

Sí

S**EE**

No

No

N**O**

Please

Por favor

P**O**R F**ah**-V**O**R

Abbreviated PFV throughout the book

Thank you

Gracias

GR**ah**´-S**EE**-**ah**S

Excuse me

Perdón   Con permiso

P**E**R-D**O**N   K**O**N P**E**R-M**EE**´-S**O**

I'm sorry

Lo siento   Perdón

L**O** S**EE**-**E**N-T**O**   P**E**R-D**O**N

I am a tourist.

Soy turista.

Soy Too-REES-Tah

I do not speak Spanish.

No hablo español.

NO ah-BLO eS-Pah-N-YOL

I speak a little Spanish.

Hablo un poco de español.

ah-BLO oon PO-KO De
eS-Pah-N-YOL

Do you understand English?

¿Entiende inglés?

eN-TEE-eN-De eN-GLeS

I don't understand!

¡No entiendo!

NO eN-TEE-eN-DO

Please repeat.

Repita, por favor.

Re-PEE-Tah POR Fah-VOR

More slowly, please.

Más despacio, por favor.

MahS DeS-Pah-SEE-O   PFV

FEELINGS

I want…

Quiero…

KEE-ĕ́-RO

I have…

Tengo…

TĚN-GO…

I know.

Yo sé.

YO SĚ

I don't know.

No sé.

NO SĚ

I like it.

Me gusta.

MĚ GOOS-Tah

I don't like it.

No me gusta.

NO MĚ GOOS-Tah

I'm lost.

Estoy perdido. (male)   Estoy perdida. (female)

ⓔS-Tⓞⓨ PⓔR-Dⓔⓔ-Dⓞ (ⓐⓗ)

I'm in a hurry.

Tengo prisa.

TⓔN-Gⓞ PRⓔⓔ-Sⓐⓗ

I'm tired.

Estoy cansado. (male) Estoy cansada. (female)

ⓔS-Tⓞⓨ KⓐⓗN-Sⓐⓗ-Dⓞ (ⓐⓗ)

I'm ill.

Estoy enfermo. (male) Estoy enferma. (female)

ⓔS-Tⓞⓨ ⓔN-FⓔR-Mⓞ (ⓐⓗ)

I'm hungry.

Tengo hambre.

TⓔN-Gⓞ ⓐⓗM-BRⓔ

I'm thirsty.

Tengo sed.

TⓔN-Gⓞ SⓔD

I'm angry.

Estoy enojado. (male)   Estoy enojada. (female)

ⓔS-Tⓞⓨ ⓔN-ⓞ-Hⓐⓗ-Dⓞ (ⓐⓗ)

EPLS displays the feminine ending in parenthesis.

INTRODUCTIONS

My name is...

Me llamo...

Mẽ Y@h-M⓪...

What's your name?

¿Cómo se llama usted?

KÓ-M⓪ Sẽ Y@h-M@h ⓞⓞS-Tẽ́D

Where are you from?

¿De dónde es usted?

Dẽ DÓN-Dẽ ẽS ⓞⓞS-Tẽ́D

Do you live here?

¿Vive usted aquí?

Vẽẽ́-Vẽ ⓞⓞS-Tẽ́D @h-Kẽẽ

I just arrived.

Acabo de llegar.

@h-K@h́-B⓪ Dẽ Yẽ-G@h́B

What hotel are you [staying] at?

¿En qué hotel está usted?

ẽN Kẽ ⓞ-Tẽ́L ẽS-T@h́ ⓞⓞS-Tẽ́D

I'm at the…hotel.

Estoy en el hotel…

ⓔS-Tⓞⓨ ⓔN ⓔL ⓞ-Tⓔ́L…

It was nice to meet you.

Mucho gusto.

Mⓞⓞ-CHⓞ Gⓞⓞ́S-Tⓞ

G is pronounced like the **g** in **g**o.

See you later.

Hasta luego.

ⓐⓗ́S-Tⓐⓗ Lⓞⓞ-Ⓐ́-Gⓞ

See you next time.

Hasta la vista.

ⓐⓗ́S-Tⓐⓗ Lⓐⓗ Vⓔⓔ́-STⓤⓗ

Good luck!

¡Buena suerte!

BWⓔ́-Nⓐⓗ SWⓔ́R-Tⓔ

You will notice that in Spanish spelling, the letter **e** is sometimes pronounced like the **e** in r**e**d and sometimes like the **a** in c**a**ke. This will vary from region to region and will not affect the understanding of the word.

THE BIG QUESTIONS

Who?

¿Quién?

KẼẼ-ẽN

Who is it?

¿Quién es?

KẼẼ-ẽN ẽS

What?

¿Qué?   ¿Cómo?

Kẽ   KŌ-MŌ

Use **¿cómo?** if you didn't hear well or want something
repeated.

What's that?

¿Qué es eso?

Kẽ ẽS ẽ-SŌ

When?

¿Cuándo?

KWahN-DŌ

Where?

¿Dónde?

DŌN-Dẽ

Where is…?

¿Dónde está…?

DON-De eS-Tah…

Which?

¿Cuál?

KWahL

Why?

¿Por qué?

POR Ke

How?

¿Cómo?

KO-MO

How much? (does it cost)

¿Cuánto?

KWahN-TO

KW sounds like the **qu** in **qu**it.

How long?

¿Cuánto tiempo?

KWahN-TO TEE-eM-PO

ASKING FOR THINGS

The following phrases are valuable for directions, food, help, etc.

I would like…

Quisiera…

K┈-S┈-ĕ-R@…

I need…

Necesito…

Nĕ-Sĕ-S┈-T⧉…

Can you…

Puede usted…

PWĕ-Dĕ ⧉S-TĕD…

When asking for things be sure to say <u>please</u> and <u>thank you</u>.

Please	**Thank you**
Por Favor	Gracias
P⧉R F@-V⧉R	GR@-S┈-@S

PHRASEMAKER

Combine **I would like** with the following phrases, and you will have an effective way to ask for things.

I would like…

Quisiera…

KEE-SEE-ē-Rah…

▸ **more coffee**

más café

MahS Kah-Fē

▸ **some water**

agua

ah-GWah

▸ **some ice**

hielo

Yē-LO

▸ **the menu**

la carta

Lah Kah'R-Tah

PHRASEMAKER

Here are a few sentences you
can use when you feel the urge
to say **I need**… or **Can you**…?

I need…

Necesito… por favor.

Nℯ-Sℯ-Sℰℰ-T◉… PFV

▸ **help**

ayuda

ⓐ-Yⓞⓞ-Dⓐ

▸ **directions**

direcciones

Dℰℰ-RℯK-Sℰℰ-◉-Nℯ S

▸ **more money**

más dinero

Mⓐ S Dℰℰ-Nℯ-R◉

▸ **change**

cambio

Kⓐ M-Bℰℰ-◉

▸ **a lawyer**

un abogado

ⓞⓞN ⓐ-B◉-Gⓐ-D◉

PHRASEMAKER

Can you…

¿Puede usted… por favor?

PW@-D@ @@S-T@D… PFV

▸ **help me?**

ayudarme?

@-Y@-D@R-M@

▸ **show me?**

enseñarme?

@N-S@N-Y@R-M@

▸ **give me…?**

darme…?

D@R-M@…

▸ **tell me…?**

decirme…?

D@-S@R-M@

▸ **take me to…?**

llevarme al…?

Y@-V@R-M@ @L…

ASKING THE WAY

No matter how independent you are, sooner or later you'll probably have to ask for directions.

Where is…?

¿Dónde está…?

DŎN-Dĕ ĕS-Tah…

Is it near?

¿Está cerca?

ĕS-Tah SĕR-Kah

Is it far?

¿Está lejos?

ĕS-Tah Lĕ-HOS

I'm looking for…

Estoy buscando...

ĕS-Toy BOOS-Kahn-DO…

I'm lost! (male)

¡Estoy perdido!

ĕS-Toy PĕR-DEE-DO

I'm lost! (female)

Estoy perdida!

ĕS-Toy PĕR-DEE-Dah

PHRASEMAKER

Where is...

¿Dónde está...

DŌN-Dē̆ ē̆S-Tah́...

▶ **the restroom?**

el baño?

ē̆L Bah́N-YŌ

▶ **the telephone?**

el teléfono?

ē̆L Tē̆-Lē̆́-FŌ-NŌ

▶ **the beach?**

la playa?

Lah PLah́-Yah

▶ **the hotel...?**

el hotel...?

ē̆L Ō-Tē̆́L...

▶ **the train for...?**

el tren para...?

ē̆L TRē̆N Pah́-Rah...

TIME

What time is it?

¿Qué hora es?

Kⓔ Ⓞ́-Rⓐh ⓔS

Morning

La mañana

Lⓐh Mⓐh-Yⓐh́-Nⓐh

Noon

El mediodía

ⓔL Mⓔ-DⒺⒺ-Ⓞ-DⒺⒺ́-ⓐh

Night

La noche

Lⓐh NⓄ́-CHⓔ

Today

Hoy

ⓞy

In Spanish spelling the **h** is always silent.

Tomorrow

Mañana

Mⓐh-Yⓐh́-Nⓐh

This week
Esta semana

ĕS-Tah Sĕ-Mah-Nah

This month
Este mes

ĕS-Tĕ MĕS

This year
Este año

ĕS-Tĕ ahN-YO

Now
Ahora

ah-O-Rah

Soon
Pronto

PRON-TO

Later
Más tarde

MahS TahR-Dĕ

Never
Nunca

NooN-Kah

WHO IS IT?

I
Yo
Y⊚

You (Formal)	**You** (Informal)
Usted	Tú
⊚S-T⁀ěD	T⊚
Use this form of **you** with people you don't know well	Use this form of **you** with people you know well

---

He	**She**
El	Ella
⁀ěL	⁀ě-Y⒜

We

Nosotros	Nosotras
N⊚-S⊚́-TR⊚S	N⊚-S⊚́-TR⒜S
Use this form for males only or males and females.	Use this form for females only.

They

Ellos	Ellas
⁀ě-Y⊚S	⁀ě-Y⒜S
A group of men only or a group of men and woman.	A group of women only.

THE, A (AN), AND SOME

To use the correct form of **The**, **A (An)**, or **Some**, you must know if the Spanish word is masculine or feminine. Often you will have to guess! If you make a mistake, you will still be understood.

The

La

L**ah**

The before a singular feminine noun:
(La) girl is pretty.

Las

L**ah**S

The before a plural feminine noun:
(Las) girls are pretty.

El

ĕL

The before a singular masculine noun:
(El) man is handsome.

Los

L**o**S

The before a plural masculine noun:
(Los) men are handsome.

A, An

Un

ooN

A or **an** before a singular masculine noun:
He is (un) man.

Una

oó-N**ah**

A or **an** before a singular feminine noun:
She is (una) woman.

Some

Unos

oó-N**o**S

Some before plural masculine nouns:
(Unos) men

Unas

oó-N**ah**S

Some before plural feminine nouns:
(Unas) women

USEFUL OPPOSITES

Near	**Far**
Cerca	Lejos
SĕR-Kah	LĕH-OS

Here	**There**
Aquí	Ahí
ah-KEE	ah-EE

Left (direction)	**Right** (direction)
Izquierda	Derecha
EES-KĕR-Dah	Dĕ-Rĕ-CHah

A little	**A lot**
Un poquito	Mucho
ooN PO-KEE-TO	Moo-CHO

More	**Less**
Más	Menos
MahS	Mĕ-NOS

Big	**Small**
Grande	Pequeño
GRahN-Dĕ	Pĕ-KĕN-YO

Open	**Closed**
Abierto	Cerrado
ah-BEE-ĕR-TO	Sĕ-Bah-DO
Cheap	**Expensive**
Barato	Caro
Bah-Bah-TO	Kah-BO
Clean	**Dirty**
Limpio	Sucio
LĔM-PEE-O	Soo-SEE-O
Good	**Bad**
Bueno	Malo
BWĕ-NO	Mah-LO
Vacant	**Occupied**
Vacantes	Ocupado
Vah-Kah'N-TĕS	O-Koo-Pah-DO
Right	**Wrong**
Correcto	Incorrecto
KO-Bĕ'K-TO	ĔN-KO-Bĕ'K-TO

WORDS OF ENDEARMENT

I love you.

Te amo.

T® @-MO

My love

Mi amor

M® @-MOR

My life

Mi vida

M® V®-D@

My friend (to a male)

Mi amigo

M® @-M®-GO

My friend (to a female)

Mi amiga

M® @-M®-G@

Kiss me!

¡Bésame!

B®-S@-M®

WORDS OF ANGER

What do you want?

¿Qué quiere usted?

K

Leave me alone!

¡Déjeme en paz!

D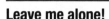

Go away!

¡Váyase!

VĪ-Yah-Sē

Stop bothering me!

¡No me moleste más!

NO MĒ MO-LĒS-TĒ MahS

Be quiet!

¡Silencio!

SEE-LĒN-SEE-O

That's enough!

¡Basta!

BahS-Tah

COMMON EXPRESSIONS

When you are at a loss for words but have the feeling you should say something, try one of these!

Who knows?

¿Quién sabe?

KEE-éN Sah-Bē

That's the truth!

¡Es verdad!

ēS VēR-DahD

Sure!

¡Claro!

KLah-RO

Wow!

¡Caramba!

Kah-RahM-Bah

What's happening?

¿Qué pasa?

Kē Pah-Sah

I think so.

Creo que sí.

KRē-O Kē SEE

Cheers!

¡Salud!

S(ah)-L(oo)D

Good luck!

¡Buena suerte!

BW(e)-N(ah) SW(e)R-T(e)

With pleasure!

¡Con mucho gusto!

K(o)N M(oo)-CH(o) G(oo)S-T(o)

My goodness!

¡Dios mío!

D(ee)-(o)S M(ee)-(o)

What a shame! / That's too bad!

¡Qué lástima!

K(e) L(ah)S-T(ee)-M(ah)

Well done! Bravo!

¡Olé!

(o)-L(a)

Never mind!

¡Olvídelo!

(o)L-V(ee)-D(e)-L(o)

USEFUL COMMANDS

Stop!

¡Párese!

Pah-Rē-Sē

Go!

¡Vaya!

Vah-Yah

Wait!

¡Espérese!

ēS-Pē-Rē-Sē

Hurry!

¡Apúrese!

ah-Poo-Rē-Sē

Slow down!

¡Despacio!

Dē-SPah-SEE-O

Come here!

¡Venga acá! (formal)   ¡Ven acá! (informal)

Vēn-Gah ah-Kah   Vēn ah-Kah

Help!

¡Socorro!

SO-KO-RO

EMERGENCIES

Fire!

¡Incendio!

ⒺN-SⒺN-DⒺ-Ⓞ

Emergency!

¡Emergencia!

Ⓔ-MⒺB-HⒺN-SⒺ-ⓐh

Call the police!

¡Llame a la policía!

Yⓐh-MⒺ ⓐh Lⓐh PⓄ-LⒺ-SⒺ-ⓐh

Call a doctor!

¡Llame un médico!

Yⓐh-MⒺ ⓄⓄN MⒺ-DⒺ-KⓄ

Call an ambulance!

¡Llame una ambulancia!

Yⓐh-MⒺ ⓄⓄ-Nⓐh
ⓐhM-BⓄⓄ-LⓐhN-SⒺ-ⓐh

I need help!

¡Necesito ayuda!

NⒺ-SⒺ-SⒺ-TⓄ ⓐh-YⓄⓄ-Dⓐh

ARRIVAL

Passing through customs should be easy since there are usually agents available who speak English. You may be asked how long you intend to stay and if you have anything to declare.

- Have your passport ready.

- Be sure all documents are up-to-date.

- While in a foreign country, it is wise to keep receipts for everything you buy.

- Be aware that many countries will charge a departure tax when you leave. Your travel agent should be able to find out if this affects you.

- If you have connecting flights, be sure to reconfirm them in advance.

- Make sure your luggage is clearly marked inside and out.

- Take valuables and medicines in carry-on bags.

SIGNS TO LOOK FOR:

ADUANA (Customs)

FRONTERA (Border)

CONTROL DE EQUIPAJE (Baggage control)

KEY WORDS

Baggage

El equipaje

ⓔL ⓔ-ⓀEE-Pah-Hⓔ

Customs

La aduana

Lah ah-DWah-Nah

Documents

Los documentos

LOS DO-Koo-MⓔN-TOS

Passport

El pasaporte

ⓔL Pah-Sah-POR-Tⓔ

Porter

El maletero   El mozo (Spain)

ⓔL Mah-Lⓔ-Tⓔ-RO   ⓔL MO-THO

In Spain the letter **z** is prounounced like the **th** in **th**ink.

Tax

Los impuestos

LOS EEM-PWⓔS-TOS

USEFUL PHRASES

Here is my passport.

Aquí tiene mi pasaporte.

@ah-KEE TEE-ĕ-Nĕ MEE
Pah-Sah-POR-Tĕ

I have nothing to declare.

No tengo nada que declarar.

NO TĕN-GO Nah-Dah
Kĕ Dĕ-KLah-Rah'R

I'm here on business.

Vengo de negocios.

VĕN-GO Dĕ Nĕ-GO-SEE-OS

I'm here on vacation.

Vengo de vacaciones.

VĕN-GO Dĕ Vah-Kah-SEE-O-Nĕs

Is there a problem?

¿Hay algún problema?

I ahL-GooN PRO-BLĕ-Mah

PHRASEMAKER

I'll be staying…

Me voy a quedar…

M̃ẽ Vⓞy ⓐh Kẽ-D̃ⓐh̃R…

▸ **one week**

una semana

ⓞⓞ-Ñⓐh Sẽ-M̃ⓐh-Ñⓐh

▸ **two weeks**

dos semanas

D̃ⓞS Sẽ-M̃ⓐh-Ñⓐh S

▸ **one month**

un mes

ⓞⓞN M̃ẽS

▸ **two months**

dos meses

D̃ⓞS M̃ẽS-ẽS

USEFUL PHRASES

I need a porter!

¡Necesito un maletero!

Nē-Sē-SĒ-TO ᴏᴏN
Mah-L-ē-Tē-RO

These are my bags.

Estas son mis maletas.

ē-S-Tahs SON MĒS Mah-Lē-Tahs

I'm missing a bag.

Me falta una maleta.

Mē Fahl-Tah ᴏᴏ-Nah Mah-Lē-Tah

Take my bags to the taxi, please.

Lleve mis maletas al taxi, por favor.

Yē-Vē MĒS Mah-Lē-Tahs ahL
Tahk-Sē POR Fah-VOR

Thank you. This is for you.

Gracias. Esto es para usted.

GRah-SĒ-ahs
ē-S-TO ēs Pah-Rah ᴏᴏS-Tēd

PHRASEMAKER

Where is…

¿Dónde está...

DÓN-Dⓔ ⓔS-Tⓐ...

▶ **customs?**

la aduana?

Lⓐ ⓐ-DWⓐ-Nⓐ

▶ **baggage claim?**

la reclamación de equipaje?

Lⓐ Rⓔ-KLⓐ-Mⓐ-SⒺ-ÓN
Dⓔ ⓔ-KⒺ-Pⓐ-Hⓔ

▶ **the money exchange?**

la casa de cambio?

Lⓐ Kⓐ-Sⓐ Dⓔ KⓐM-BⒺ-Ⓞ

▶ **the taxi stand?**

la parada de taxis?

Lⓐ Pⓐ-Rⓐ-Dⓐ Dⓔ Tⓐ-SⒺS

▶ **the bus stop?**

la parada de autobuses?

Lⓐ-Pⓐ-Rⓐ-Dⓐ Dⓔ
ⓞw-TⓞB-Bⓞ-SⓔS

HOTEL SURVIVAL

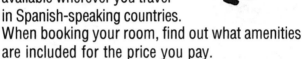

A wide selection of accommodations, ranging from the most basic to the most extravagant, are available wherever you travel in Spanish-speaking countries. When booking your room, find out what amenities are included for the price you pay.

- Make reservations well in advance and get written confirmation of your reservations before you leave home.

- Always have identification ready when checking in.

- Do not leave valuables, prescriptions, or cash in your room when you are not there!

- Electrical items like blow-dryers may need an adapter. Your hotel may be able to provide one, but to be safe, take one with you.

- Although a service charge is usually included on your bill, it is customary to tip maids, bellhops, and doormen.

KEY WORDS

Hotel

El hotel

ĔL Ō-TĔL

Bellman

El botones

ĔL BŌ-TŌ-NĔS

Maid

La camarera

Lah Kah-Mah-RĔ-Rah

Message

El recado

ĔL RĔ-Kah-DŌ

Reservation

La reservación

Lah RĔ-SĔR-Vah-SEE-ŌN

Room service

El servicio de habitación

ĔL SĔR-VEE-SEE-Ō DĔ
ah-BEE-Tah-SEE-ŌN

CHECKING IN

My name is…

Me llamo…

M⑥ Y⑳-M⑥…

I have a reservation.

Tengo una reservación.

T⑥N-G⑥ ⑳-N⑳
R⑥-S⑥R-V⑳-S⑥⑥-Ó'N

If you don't have a reservation, just say no before
this phrase.

Have you any vacancies?

¿Tiene alguna habitación libre?

T⑥⑥-⑥'-N⑥ ⑳L-G⑳-N⑳
⑳-B⑥⑥-T⑳-S⑥⑥-Ó'N L⑥⑥-BR⑥

What is the charge per night?

¿Cuánto es por noche?

KW⑳N-T⑥ ⑥S P⑥R N⑥'-CH⑥

Is there room service?

¿Hay servicio de habitación?

⑥ S⑥R-V⑥⑥'-S⑥⑥-⑥ D⑥
⑳-B⑥⑥-T⑳-S⑥⑥-Ó'N

PHRASEMAKER

I would like a room...

Quiero un cuarto… por favor

KEE-ĕ́-RO ōN KWah-R-TO… PFV

▸ **with a bath**

con un baño

KON ōN Bah́N-YO

▸ **with one bed**

con una cama

KON ōó-Nah Kah́-Mah

▸ **with two beds**

con dos camas

KON DOS Kah́-MahS

▸ **with a shower**

con una ducha

KON ōó-Nah Dōó-CHah

▸ **with a view**

con una vista

KON ōó-Nah VEÉS-Tah

USEFUL PHRASES

Where is the dining room?

¿Dónde está el comedor?

DON-De eS-Tah eL
KO-Me-DOR

Are meals included?

¿Están las comidas incluidas?

eS-TaN LahS KO-MEE-DahS
EEN-KLoo-EE-DahS

What time is breakfast?

¿A qué hora es el desayuno?

ah Ke O-Rah eS eL
De-Sah-Yoo-NO

What time is lunch?

¿A qué hora es la comida?

ah Ke O-Rah eS Lah
KO-MEE-Dah

What time is dinner?

¿A qué hora es la cena?

ah Ke O-Rah eS
Lah Se-Nah

My room key, please.

Mi llave de mi cuarto, por favor.

MEE YAH-VE DE MEE
KWAHR-TO PFV

Are there any messages for me?

¿Tengo algún recado?

TEN-GO AHL-GOON RE-KAH-DO

Please wake me at...

Me despierta a las...por favor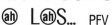

ME DES-PEE-ER-TAH
AH LAHS... PFV

6:00	6:30
seis	seis y media
SAS	SAS EE ME-DEE-ah

7:00	7:30
siete	siete y media
SEE-e-TE	SEE-e-TE EE ME-DEE-ah

8:00	8:30
ocho	ocho y media
O-CHO	O-CHO EE ME-DEE-ah

9:00	9:30
nueve	nueve y media
NWE-VE	NWE-VE EE ME-DEE-ah

PHRASEMAKER

I need...

Necesito...

NĕĚ-SĕĚ-SĒĒ-TŌ...

▸ **a babysitter**

una niñera

ŌŌ-Nah NĒĒN-Yĕ-Rah

▸ **a bellman**

un botones

ŌŌN BŌ-TŌ-NĕS

▸ **more blankets**

más cobijas (mantas)

Mah S KŌ-BĒĒ-Hah S (Mah N-Tah S)

▸ **a hotel safe**

una caja fuerte

ŌŌ-Nah Kah-Hah FWĕR-Tĕ

▸ **ice cubes**

cubitos de hielo

KŌŌ-BĒĒ-TŌS Dĕ Yĕ-LŌ

▶ **an extra key**

otra llave

Ō-TRah   Yah́-Vē

▶ **a maid**

una camarera

ōō-Nah   Kah-Mah-Rē-Rah

▶ **the manager**

el gerente

ēL   Hē-Rēń-Tē

▶ **clean sheets**

sábanas limpias

Sah́-Bah-NahS   LEEM-PEE-ahS

▶ **soap**

jabón

Hah-BṒN

▶ **toilet paper**

papel higiénico

Pah-PēL   EE-HEE-ē-NEE-KO

▶ **more towels**

más toallas

MahS   TO-ah-YahS

PHRASEMAKER
(PROBLEMS)

There is no…

No hay…

NŌ Ī…

▶ **electricity**

electricidad

ē-LēK-TRēē-Sēē-DahD

▶ **heat**

calefacción

Kah-Lē-Fah-K-Sēē-ŌN

▶ **hot water**

agua caliente

ah-GWah Kah-Lēē-ēN-Tē

▶ **light**

luz

LūūS

▶ **toilet paper**

papel higiénico

Pah-PēL ēē-Hēē-ē-Nēē-KŌ

PHRASEMAKER
(SPECIAL NEEDS)

Do you have…

¿Tiene…

T@-@́-N@…

▶ **an elevator?**

un ascensor?

@N @-S@N-S@́R

▶ **a ramp?**

una rampa?

@́-N@ R@M-P@

▶ **a wheel chair?**

una silla de ruedas?

@́-N@ S@́-Y@ D@ R@-@́-D@S

▶ **facilities for the disabled?**

facilidades para los inválidos?

F@-S@-L@-D@́-D@S P@́-R@ L@S
@N-V@́-L@-D@S

CHECKING OUT

The bill, please.

La cuenta, por favor.

L@h KW@N-T@h PFV

Is this bill correct?

¿Está bien la cuenta?

@S-T@h B@-@N L@h KW@N-T@h

Do you accept credit cards?

¿Se aceptan tarjetas de crédito?

S@ @h-S@P-T@N T@R-H@-T@S
D@ KR@-D@-T@

Could you have my luggage brought down?

¿Pueden bajarme el equipaje?

PW@-D@N B@h-H@R-M@ @L
@-K@-P@h-H@

Can you call a taxi for me?

¿Puede llamarme un taxi?

PWĔ-DĔ Yah-MahR-MĔ
ooN TahK-SEE

I had a very good time!

¡Me lo pasé muy bien!

MĔ LO Pah-SĔ MWEE BEE-ĔN

Thanks for everything.

Gracias por todo.

GRah-SEE-ahS POR TO-DO

We'll see you next time.

Nos veremos la próxima.

NOS VĔ-RĔ-MOS Lah
PROK-SEE-Mah

Good-bye.

Adiós.

ah-DEE-OS

RESTAURANT SURVIVAL

The food available in Latin America and Spain is diverse. You will find a variety of tasty regional specialties. Mealtimes may be quite different than what you are used to!

- In Latin America and Spain, breakfast is usually served till 11 AM, lunch between 1 and 4 PM, and dinner from 9 PM till midnight. These are general guidelines and vary from country to country.

- In Spain, the Tasca bar offers appetizers or (**tapas**), a delicious way to fill the gap of time between lunch and dinner and a great way to meet people.

- A tip or service charge is often automatically included in your bill. Look for the words **Servicio Incluido**.

- In Mexico, avoid drinking tap water. Bottled water is available and recommended. In major hotels and restaurants, purified water is used; however, it is advisable to ask if your drink and or ice has been prepared with tap water.

KEY WORDS

Breakfast

El desayuno

ⒺL DⒺS-ⓐ-Yⓞⓞ-Nⓞ

Lunch

El almuerzo

ⒺL ⓐL-MWⒺB-Sⓞ

Dinner

La cena

Lⓐ SⒺ-Nⓐ

Waiter

El camarero

ⒺL Kⓐ-Mⓐ-BⒺ-Bⓞ

Waitress

La camarera

Lⓐ Kⓐ-Mⓐ-BⒺ-Bⓐ

Restaurant

El restaurante

ⒺL BⒺS-Tⓞⓦ-Bⓐⓝ-TⒺ

USEFUL PHRASES

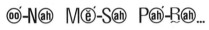

A table for...

Una mesa para...

ⓞⓞ-Nⓐⓗ Mⓔ-Sⓐⓗ Pⓐⓗ-Rⓐⓗ...

2	4	6
dos	cuatro	seis
DⓞS	KWⓐⓗ-TRⓞ	Sⓐ S

The menu, please.

La carta, por favor.

Lⓐⓗ KⓐⓗR-Tⓐⓗ PFV

Separate checks, please.

Cuentas separadas, por favor.

KWⓔN-TⓐⓗS Sⓔ-Pⓐⓗ-Rⓐⓗ-DⓐⓗS PFV

We are in a hurry.

Tenemos prisa.

Tⓔ-Nⓔ-MⓞS PRⓔⓔ-Sⓐⓗ

What do you recommend?

¿Qué recomienda la casa?

Kⓔ Rⓔ-Kⓞ-Mⓔⓔ-ⓔN-Dⓐⓗ

Lⓐⓗ Kⓐⓗ-Sⓐⓗ

Please bring me...

Tráigame... por favor

TRŌ-Gah-Mē... PFV

Please bring us...

Tráiganos... por favor

TRŌ-Gah-NOS... PFV

I'm hungry.

Tengo hambre.

TĒN-GO ahM-BRē

I'm thirsty.

Tengo sed.

TĒN-GO SēD

Is service included?

¿Está incluido el servicio?

ēS-Tah ēEN-KLOO-ēE-DO ēL
SēR-Vēē-Sēē-O

The bill, please.

La cuenta, por favor.

Lah KWēN-Tah PFV

In Spain, the menu prices are required by law to include the
service charge. It is customary to leave an additional tip if
you are happy with the service!

PHRASEMAKER

Ordering beverages is easy and a great way to practice your Spanish! In many foreign countries you will have to request ice with your drinks.

Please bring me…

Tráigame... por favor.

TRĪ-G@h-M@̃... PFV

▸ **coffee**

un café

@N K@h-F@̃

▸ **tea**

un té

@N T@̃

▸ **with cream**

con crema

K@N KR@̃-M@h

▸ **with sugar**

con azúcar

K@N @h-S@@-K@hR

▸ **with lemon**

con limón

K@N L@@-M@́N

▸ **with ice**

con hielo

K@N Y@̃-L@

Soft drinks

Los refrescos

LOS RĒ-FRĒS-KOS

Milk

La leche

Lah LĒ-CHĒ

Hot chocolate

El chocolate caliente

ĒL CHO-KO-Lah-TĒ Kah-LEE-ĒN-TĒ

Juice

El jugo

ĒL HOO-GO

Orange juice

El jugo de naranja

ĒL HOO-GO DĒ Nah-Rah-N-Hah

Ice water

El agua fría

ĒL ah-GWah FRĒE-ah

Mineral water

El agua mineral

ĒL ah-GWah MEE-NĒ-Rah-L

AT THE BAR

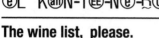

Bartender

El cantinero

ⓔL Kⓐ︎N-Tⓔ︎E-Nⓔ︎-ℝⓄ

The wine list, please.

La lista de vinos, por favor.

Lⓐ︎ Lⓔ︎E'S-Tⓐ︎ Dⓔ︎ Vⓔ︎E'-NⓄs PFV

Cocktail

El cóctel

ⓔL KⓄK-Tⓔ︎L

On the rocks

Con hielo

KⓄN Yⓔ︎-LⓄ

Straight

Sin hielo

Sⓔ︎EN Yⓔ︎-LⓄ

With lemon

Con limón

KⓄN Lⓔ︎E-MⓄ'N

PHRASEMAKER

I would like a glass of…

Quisiera un vaso de…

KEE-SEE-é-Rah ON Vah-SO Dé…

▶ **champagne**

champaña

CHahM-Pah'N-Yah

▶ **beer**

cerveza

SéR-Vé-Sah

▶ **wine**

vino

VEE-NO or BEE-NO

You will often hear the Spanish letter **v** pronounced like a soft English **b**.

▶ **red wine**

vino tinto

VEE-NO TEE'N-TO

▶ **white wine**

vino blanco

VEE-NO BLahN-KO

ORDERING BREAKFAST

In Latin America, breakfast can be extravagant. In Spain, breakfast is generally a simple meal consisting of coffee or tea and bread.

Bread

El pan

ⓔL Pⓐ N

Toast

El pan tostado

ⓔL Pⓐ N Tⓞ-STⓐ-Dⓞ

with butter

con mantequilla

Kⓞ N Mⓐ N-Tⓔ-KⒺ-Yⓐ

with jam

con mermelada

Kⓞ N Mⓔ R-Mⓔ-Lⓐ-Dⓐ

Cereal

El cereal

ⓔL Sⓔ-Rⓔ-ⓐL

PHRASEMAKER

I would like…

Quisiera…

KEE-SEE-é-Rah…

▶ **two eggs…**

dos huevos…

DOS Wé-VOS…

▶ **scrambled**   ▶ **fried**

revueltos   fritos

Ré-VWéL-TOS   FREE-TOS

▶ **with bacon**

con tocino

KON TO-SEE-NO

▶ **with ham**

con jamón

KON Hah-MON

▶ **with potatoes**

con papas   con patatas (Spain)

KON Pah-Pah S   KON Pah-Tah-Tah S

LUNCH AND DINNER

Although you are encouraged to sample regional cuisines, it is important to be able to order foods you are familiar with. This section will provide phrases to help you.

I would like…

Quisiera…

KEE-SEE-ē-Rah…

We would like…

Quisiéramos…

KEE-SEE-ē-Rah-MOS

Bring us…

Nos trae... por favor.

NOS TRĪ-ē… kk

The lady would like…

La señora quisiera…

Lah SēN-YO-Rah KEE-SEE-ē-Rah…

The gentleman would like…

El señor quisiera…

ēL SēN-YOR KEE-SEE-ē-Rah…

STARTERS

Appetizers

Los entremeses

LOS ĕN-TRĕ-Mĕ-SĕS

Bread and butter

El pan y la mantequilla

ĕL PahN EE Lah MahN-Tĕ-KEE-Yah

Cheese

El queso

ĕL Kĕ-SO

Fruit

La fruta

Lah FROO-Tah

Salad

La ensalada

Lah ĕN-Sah-Lah-Dah

Soup

La sopa

Lah SO-Pah

MEATS

Bacon

El tocino

ⓔL Tⓞ-SⒺⒺ-Nⓞ

Beef

La carne de res

Lⓐ Kⓐ'R-Nⓔ Dⓔ RⓔS

Beef steak

El bistec

ⓔL BⒺⒺ-STⓔK

Ham

El jamón

ⓔL Hⓐ-MⓞN

Lamb

El cordero

ⓔL KⓞR-Dⓔ'-Rⓞ

Pork

La carne de puerco   Las carnitas (Mexico)

Lⓐ Kⓐ'R-Nⓔ Dⓔ PWⓔR-Kⓞ

LⓐS Kⓐ'R-NⒺⒺ-TⓐS

Veal

La carne de ternera

Lⓐ Kⓐ'R-Nⓔ Dⓔ TⓔR-Nⓔ'-Rⓐ

POULTRY

Baked chicken

El pollo al horno

ⒺL PⓄ́-YⓄ ⓐL Ⓞ́R-NⓄ

Broiled chicken

El pollo a la parrilla

ⒺL PⓄ́-YⓄ ⓐ Lⓐ Pⓐ-RⒺ́E-Yⓐ

Fried chicken

El pollo frito

ⒺL PⓄ́-YⓄ FRⒺE-TⓄ

Duck

El pato

ⒺL Pⓐ́-TⓄ

Goose

El ganso

ⒺL Gⓐ́N-SⓄ

Turkey

El pavo   El guajolote (Mexico)

ⒺL Pⓐ́-VⓄ   ⒺL GWⓐ-HⓄ-LⓄ́-TⒺ

SEAFOOD

Fish

El pescado

ⒺL PⒺS-Kⓐ-DⓄ

Lobster

La langosta

Lⓐ LⓐN-GⓄ-STⓐ

Oysters

Las ostras

LⓐS ⓄS-TRⓐS

Salmon

El salmón

ⒺL SⓐL-MⓄN

Shrimp

Los camarones

LⓄS Kⓐ-Mⓐ-RⓄ-NⒺS

Trout

La trucha

Lⓐ TRⓄⓄ-CHⓐ

Tuna

El atún

ⒺL ⓐ-TⓄⓄN

OTHER ENTREES

Sandwich

La torta (Latin America)   El bocadillo (Spain)

Lah TOR-Tah   eL BO-Kah-DEE-YO

Hot dog

El hot dog

eL Hah T DahG

Hamburger

La hamburguesa

Lah ah M-BooB-Ge-Sah

French fries

Las papas fritas or Las patatas fritas (Spain)

Lah S Pah-Pah S FREE-Tah S

Lah S Pah-Tah-Tah S FREE-Tah S

Pasta

La pasta

Lah Pah S-Tah

Pizza

La pizza

Lah PEE-Sah

VEGETABLES

Carrots

Las zanahorias

L(ah)S   S(ah)-N(ah)-O-R(EE)-(ah)S

Corn

El maíz

(e)L   M(ah)-(EE)S

Mushrooms

Los hongos   Los champiñones (Spain)

L(O)S   (O)N-G(O)S   L(O)S   CH(ah)M-P(EE)N-Y(O)-N(e)S

Onions

Las cebollas

L(ah)S   S(e)-B(O)-Y(ah)S

Potato

La papa   La patata (Spain)

L(ah)   P(ah)-P(ah)   L(ah)   P(ah)-T(ah)-T(ah)

Rice

El arroz

(e)L   (ah)-R(O)S

Tomato

El tomate

(e)L   T(O)-M(ah)-T(e)

FRUITS

Apple

La manzana

Lah Mahn-Sah-Nah

Banana

La banana

Lah Bah-Nah-Nah

Grapes

Las uvas

Lahs oo-Vahs

Lemon

El limón

ēl Lee-Mon

Orange

La naranja

Lah Nah-Rahn-Hah

Strawberry

La fresa

Lah Frē-Sah

Watermelon

La sandía

Lah Sahn-Dee-ah

DESSERT

Desserts
Los Postres

LOS POS-TRĕS

Apple pie
El pastel de manzana

ĕL Pah-STĕL Dĕ Mahn-Sah-Nah

Cherry pie
El pastel de cereza

ĕL Pah-STĕL Dĕ Sĕ-Rĕ-Sah

Pastries
Los pasteles

LOS Pah-STĕ-Lĕs

Candy
Los dulces

LOS DⁿⁿL-Sĕs

Ice cream

La nieve   El helado (Spain)

L@h NEE-ê-Vê   @L ê-L@h-DO

Ice-cream cone

El barquillo de helado

@L B@R-KEE-YO Dê ê-L@h-DO

Chocolate

El chocolate

@L CHO-KO-L@h-Tê

Strawberry

La fresa

L@h FRê-S@h

Vanilla

La vainilla

L@h VI-NEE-Y@h

CONDIMENTS

Butter

La mantequilla

L@h M@N-T®-K€€-Y@h

Ketchup

El ketchup

®L K®-CH@P

Mayonnaise

La mayonesa

L@h M@h-Y©-N®-S@h

Mustard

La mostaza

L@h M©S-T@h-S@h

Salt   **Pepper**

La sal   La pimienta

L@h S@hL   L@h P€€-M€€-®N-T@h

Sugar

El azúcar

®L @h-S@@-K@hB

Vinegar and oil

El vinagre y aceite

®L V€€-N@h-GB® €€ @h-S@-T®

SETTINGS

A cup
Una taza

 OO-Nah Tah-Sah

A glass
Un vaso

OON Vah-SO

A spoon
Una cuchara

OO-Nah KOO-CHah-Rah

A fork
Un tenedor

OON Tē-Nē-DOR

A knife
Un cuchillo

OON KOO-CHEE-YO

A plate
Un plato

OON PLah-TO

A napkin
Una servilleta

OO-Nah SēR-VEE-Yē-Tah

HOW DO YOU WANT IT COOKED?

Baked

Al horno

@L OR-NO

Broiled

A la parrilla

@ L@ P@-BEE-Y@

Steamed

Al vapor

@L V@-POR

Fried

Frito

FREE-TO

Rare

Poco cocida

PO-KO KO-SEE-D@

Medium

Término medio

TER-MEE-NO ME-DEE-O

Well done

Bien cocida

BEE-eN KO-SEE-D@

PROBLEMS

I didn't order this.

No pedí esto.

NŎ Pĕ-DĒ ĕS-TŎ

Is the bill correct?

¿Está bien la cuenta?

ĕS-Täh BĒ-ĕN Läh KWĕN-Täh

Please bring me...

Tráigame... por favor.

TRĪ-Gäh-Mĕ... PFV

GETTING AROUND

Getting around in a foreign country can be an adventure in itself! Taxi and bus drivers do not always speak English, so it is essential to be able to give simple directions. The words and phrases in this chapter will help you get where you're going.

- Negotiate the fare with your taxi driver in advance so there are no misunderstandings. Tell him where you want to go and find out exactly what he intends to charge.

- Never get in unmarked taxi cabs no matter where you are!

- Check with your travel agent about special rail passes which allow unlimited travel within a set period of time.

- If you are traveling by train in Europe, remember trains leave on time. Arrive early to allow time for ticket purchasing and checking in.

- There are several types of train transportation from **Talgos** (fast) to **Rápidos** (regular) and **Estrellas** (nighttime). **Regionales** travel regionally, **Cercanas** are local commuter trains, and **Largo** are long-distance trains.

KEY WORDS

Airport

El aeropuerto

ĔL ah-ĕ-RO-PWĔR-TO

Bus Station / Stop

La estación de autobuses
La parada de autobuses

Lah ĕ-STah-SEE-ŎN Dĕ ow-TO-Boo-SĕS

Lah Pah-Rah-Dah Dĕ ow-TO-Boo-SĕS

Car Rental Agency

Una agencia de carros de alquiler

ooN-ah ah-HĔN-SEE-ah Dĕ

Kah-ROS Dĕ ah-KEE-LĕR

Subway Station

La estación de metro

Lah ĕ-STah-SEE-ŎN Dĕ Mĕ-TRO

Taxi Stand

La parada de taxis

Lah Pah-Rah-Dah Dĕ Tah K-SEE

Train Station

La estación de ferrocarriles

Lah ĕ-STah-SEE-ŎN Dĕ

Fĕ-RO-Kah-REEL-ĕS

AIR TRAVEL

Arrivals
Las llegadas

L@S Y@-G@-D@S

Departures
Las salidas

L@S S@-L@-D@S

Flight number
El número de vuelo

@L N@-M@-R@ D@ VW@-L@

Airline
La línea aérea

L@ L@-N@-@ @-@-R@-@

The gate
La puerta

L@ PW@R-T@

Information
Información

@N-F@R-M@-S@-@N

Ticket (airline)
El boleto

@L B@-L@-T@

Reservations
Las reservaciones

L@S R@-S@R-V@-S@-@-N@S

PHRASEMAKER

I would like a seat…

Quisiera un asiento…

KEE-SEE-ĕ́-Rah ooN ah-SEE-ĕ́N-TO…

▶ **in first class**

en la sección de primera clase

ĕN Lah SĕK-SEE-ÓN Dĕ
PREE-Mĕ́-Rah KLah́-Sĕ

▶ **next to the window**

cerca de la ventanilla

SĕŔ-Kah Dĕ Lah VĕN-Tah-NEÉ-Yah

▶ **on the aisle**

en el pasillo

ĕN ĕL Pah-SEÉ-YO

▶ **near the exit**

cerca de la salida

SĕŔ-Kah Dĕ Lah Sah-LEÉ-Dah

BY BUS

Bus

El autobús   El camión (Mexico)

ⒺL ⓄⓌ-TⓄ-BⓄⓄ́S   ⒺL KⓐⒽ-MⒺⒺ-ⓄŃ

Where is the bus stop?

¿Dónde está la parada de autobuses?

DⓄŃ-DⒺ ⒺS-TⒶ́ Lⓐ

Pⓐ-Rⓐ́-Dⓐ DⒺ ⓄⓌ-TⓄ-BⓄⓄ́-SⒺS

Do you go to…?

¿Va usted a…?

Vⓐ ⓄⓄ-STⒺ́D ⓐ…

What is the fare?

¿Cuál es la tarifa?

KWⓐL ⒺS Lⓐ Tⓐ-RⒺⒺ́-Fⓐ

Do I need exact change?

¿Necesito tener cambio exacto?

NⒺ-SⒺ-SⒺⒺ́-TⓄ TⒺ-NⒺ́R

KⓐM-BⒺⒺ-Ⓞ ⒺK-SⓐK-TⓄ

How often do the buses run?

¿Cada cuándo pasan los autobuses?

KⒶ́-Dⓐ KWⒶ́N-DⓄ Pⓐ-SⒶ́N

LⓄS ⓄⓌ-TⓄ-BⓄⓄ́-SⒺS

PHRASEMAKER

Please tell me…

Dígame... por favor.

DĒĒ-Gah-Mē... PFV

▶ **which bus goes to…**

cuál autobús va para…

KWah L ow-TO-Boo S Vah Pah-Rah…

▶ **at what time does the bus leave**

a qué hora sale el autobús

ah Kē O-Rah Sah-Lē
ēL ow-TO-Boo S

▶ **where the bus stop is**

dónde está la parada de autobuses

DON-Dē ēS-Tah Lah Pah-Rah-Dah
Dē ow-TO-Boo-Sēs

▶ **when we are at…**

cuando estemos en…

KWahN-DO ēS-Tē-MOS ēN…

▶ **where to get off**

dónde debo bajarme

DON-Dē Dē-BO Bah-HahR-Mē

BY CAR

Fill it up.

Llénelo.

Y℮́-N℮-LO

Can you help me?

¿Puede usted ayudarme?

PW℮́-D℮   ⓞⓞS-T℮́D

@h-Yⓞⓞ-D@hR-M℮

My car won't start.

Mi carro no arranca.

M℮℮   K@h-RO   NO   @h-R@hN-K@h

Can you fix it?

¿Pueden arreglarlo?

PW℮́-D℮N   @h-R℮-GL@hR-LO

What will it cost?

¿Cuánto costará?

KW@hN-TO   KO-ST@h-R@h́

How long will it take?

¿Cuánto tiempo durará?

KW@hN-TO   T℮℮-℮M-PO   Dⓞⓞ-R@h-R@h́

PHRASEMAKER

Please check…

Revise… por favor.

Rē-VĒ-Sē… PFV

▶ **the battery**

la batería

Lah Bah-Tē-Rēē-ah

▶ **the brakes**

los frenos

LOS FRĒ-NOS

▶ **the oil**

el aceite

ĒL ah-SĀ-Tē

▶ **the tires**

las llantas

Lahs Yah'N-Tahs

▶ **the water**

el agua

ĒL ah'-GWah

SUBWAYS AND TRAINS

Where is the subway station?

¿Dónde está el metro?

DÓN-Dĕ   ĕS-Tah   ĕL   Mĕ-TRO

Where is the train station?

¿Dónde está la estación de ferrocarril?

DÓN-Dĕ   ĕS-Tah   Lah
ĕS-Tah-SEE-ÓN   Dĕ   Fĕ-RO-Kah-REĔL

A one-way ticket, please.

Un billete de ida, por favor.

ooN   BEE-Yĕ-Tĕ   Dĕ   EE-Dah   PFV

A round trip ticket

Un billete de ida y vuelta

ooN   BEE-Yĕ-Tĕ   Dĕ   EE-Dah
EE   VWĕL-Tah   PFV

First class

Primera clase

PREE-Mĕ-Rah   KLah-Sĕ

Second class

Segunda clase

Sĕ-GooN-Dah   KLah-Sĕ

Which train do I take to go to...

¿Cuál tren tomo para ir a...?

KW@L TR@N T@-M@
P@-R@ @R @...

What is the fare?

¿Cuánto es la tarifa?

KW@N-T@ @S L@ T@-R@-F@

Is this seat taken?

¿Está ocupado este asiento?

@S-T@ @-K@-P@-D@
@S-T@ @-S@-@N-T@

Do I have to change trains?

¿Tengo que cambiar de tren?

T@N-G@ K@ K@M-B@-@R
D@ TR@N

Does this train stop at...?

¿Se para este tren en...?

S@ P@-R@ @S-T@ TR@N @N...

Where are we?

¿Dónde estamos?

D@N-D@ @S-T@-M@S

BY TAXI

Can you call a taxi for me?

¿Me puede llamar un taxi?

Mē PWē-Dē Yah-Mahᴿ
ⓞⓞN Tah-K-Sēē

Are you available?

¿Está usted libre?

ēS-Tah ⓞⓞS-TēD Lēē-BRē

I want to go…

Quiero ir…

Kēē-ē-Rⓞ ēēR…

Stop here, please.

Pare aquí, por favor.

Pah-Rē ah-Kēē PFV

Please wait.

Espérese, por favor.

ē-SPē-Rē-Sē PFV

How much do I owe?

¿Cuánto le debo?

KWahN-Tⓞ Lē Dē-Bⓞ

PHRASEMAKER

I would like to go…

Quisiera ir…

K(EE)-S(EE)-(e)-R(ah)   (EE)R…

▸ **to this address**

a esta dirección

(ah)   (e)S-T(ah)   D(EE)-R(e)K-S(EE)-(O)N

▸ **to the airport**

al aeropuerto

(ah)L   (ah)-(e)-R(O)-PW(e)R-T(O)

▸ **to the bank**

al banco

(ah)L   B(ah)N-K(O)

▸ **to the hotel**

al hotel

(ah)L   (O)-T(e)L

▸ **to the hospital**

al hospital

(ah)L   (O)S-P(EE)-T(ah)L

▸ **to the subway station**

al metro

(ah)L   M(e)-TR(O)

SHOPPING

Whether you plan a major shopping
spree or just need to purchase
some basic necessities, the
following information is useful.

- In Latin America and Spain,
  shops generally close in the
  afternoon for siesta. They re-
  open in the late afternoon and stay open
  into the night.

- You are likely to encounter an item called VAT
  (in Mexico IVA). This stands for Value-Added
  Tax. It is a tax which is quoted in the price
  of merchandise and services. Unlike other
  countries, Mexico's IVA is not refundable.

- In Spain, always inquire about VAT refund
  procedures at the time of purchase.

- Always keep receipts for everything you buy!
  This will be helpful in filling out Customs
  declaration forms when you return home.

SIGNS TO LOOK FOR:

ALMACEN (Department Store)

BAZAR (Department Store, Spain)

PANADERIA (Bakery)

MERCADO (Market)

SUPERMERCADO (Supermarket)

KEY WORDS

Credit card

La tarjeta de crédito

Lⓐⓗ Tⓐⓡ-Hⓔ́-Tⓐⓗ Dⓔ Kⓡⓔ́-Dⓔⓔ-Tⓞ

Money

El dinero

ⓔL Dⓔⓔ-Nⓔ́-ⓡO

Receipt

El recibo

ⓔL ⓡⓔ́-Sⓔⓔ́-ⒷO

Sale

La venta

Lⓐⓗ Vⓔ́N-Tⓐⓗ

Store

La tienda

Lⓐⓗ Tⓔⓔ-ⓔ́N-Dⓐⓗ

Traveler's check

El cheque de viajero

ⓔL CHⓔ́-Kⓔ Dⓔ Vⓔⓔ-ⓐⓗ-Hⓔ́-ⓡO

USEFUL PHRASES

Do you sell…?

¿Vende usted…?

VeN-De ⊗S-TeD…

Do you have…?

¿Tiene usted…?

TẼ-e-Ne ⊗S-TeD…

I want to buy…

Quisiera comprar…

KẼ-SẼ-e-Rah KOM-PRahR…

How much?

¿Cuánto es?

KWahN-TO eS

When are the shops open?

¿Cuándo se abren las tiendas?

KWahN-DO Se ah-BReN
LahS TẼ-eN-DahS

No thank you.

No, gracias.

NO GRah-SẼ-ahS

I´m just looking.

Sólo estoy mirando.

SO-LO eS-Toy MEE-Bah-N-DO

It's very expensive!

¡Es muy caro!

eS MWEE Kah-BO

Can't you give me a discount?

¿No me da una rebaja?

NO Me Dah oo-Nah Be-Bah-Hah

I'll take it!

¡Me lo llevo!

Me LO Ye-VO

I'd like a receipt, please.

Quiero un recibo, por favor.

KEE-e-BO ooN Be-See-BO PFV

I want to return this.

Quiero devolver esto.

KEE-e-BO De-VOL-Ve'B e'S-TO

It doesn't fit.

No me viene.

NO Me VEE-e-Ne

PHRASEMAKER

I'm looking for…

Busco…

B⊚S-K⊙…

▸ **a bakery**

una panadería

⊚-N@h P@h-N@h-D@-R@-@h

▸ **a bank**

un banco

⊚N B@N-K⊙

▸ **a barber shop**

una peluquería

⊚-N@h P@-L⊚-K@-R@-@h

▸ **a beauty shop**

un salón de belleza

⊚N S@h-L⊙N D@ B@-Y@-S@h

▸ **a camera shop**

una tienda de fotografía

⊚N-@h T@-@N-D@h D@

F⊙-T⊙-GR@h-F@-@h

▸ **a pharmacy**

una farmacia

⊚-N@h F@R-M@h-S@-@h

PHRASEMAKER

Do you sell...

Vende usted…

VÉN-DÉ ⓞⓞS-TÉD…

▸ **aspirin?**

aspirinas?

ⓐⓗ-SPEE-REE-NⓐⓗS

▸ **cigarettes?**

cigarrillos?

SEE-Gⓐⓗ-REE-YOS

▸ **deodorant?**

desodorante?

DÉ-SO-DO-RⓐⓗN-TÉ

▸ **dresses?**

vestidos?

VÉ-STEE-DOS

▸ **film?**

rollo de cámara?

RO-YO DÉ Kⓐⓗ-Mⓐⓗ-Rⓐⓗ

▶ **pantyhose?**

pantimedias?

P@N-T€€-M€-D€€-@S

▶ **perfume?**

perfume?

P€R-F⊚-M€

▶ **razor blades?**

hojas de afeitar?

⊙-H@S D€ @-F€-T@R

▶ **shampoo?**

champú?

CH@M-P⊚

▶ **shaving cream?**

crema de afeitar?

KR€-M@ D€ @-F€-T@R

▶ **shirts?**

camisas?

K@-M€€-S@S

▶ **soap?**

jabón?

H@-B⊙N

▸ **sunglasses?**

anteojos para el sol?

ahN-Tē-O-HOS Pah-Rah ēL SOL

▸ **sunscreen?**

aceite para broncear?

ah-SA-Tē Pah-Rah
BRON-Sē-ahR

▸ **toothbrushes?**

cepillos de dientes?

Sē-Pē-YOS Dē Dē-ēN-Tēs

▸ **toothpaste?**

pasta de dientes?

PahS-Tah Dē Dē-ēN-Tēs

▸ **water?** (bottled)

agua de botella?

ah-GWah Dē BO-Tē-Yah

▸ **water?** (mineral)

agua mineral?

ah-GWah Mē-Nē-RahL

ESSENTIAL SERVICES

THE BANK

As a traveler in a foreign country your primary contact with banks will be to exchange money.

- Change enough funds before leaving home to pay for tips, food, and transportation to your final destination.

- It is also best to bring US dollar or Euro traveler's checks as well as some currency in cash. You can exchange money in banks or **Casas de Cambio.**

- Current exchange rates are posted in banks and published daily in city newspapers.

- ATM machines are readily available in Mexico and are always open. Try to use ATMs in daylight hours. Credit cards are accepted widely.

- ATM machines are readily available in Spain and a good place to obtain Euros. Credit cards are accepted and purchases usually provide a favorable rate of exchange.

KEY WORDS

Bank

El banco

ⓔL Bⓐ̃N-Kⓞ

Exchange office

La casa de cambio

Lⓐ Kⓐ́-Sⓐ Dⓔ Kⓐ̃M-BⒺⒺ-ⓞ

Money

El dinero

ⓔL DⒺⒺ-Nⓔ́-Rⓞ

Money order

El giro postal

ⓔL HⒺⒺ́-Rⓞ PⓞS-Tⓐ́L

Travelers checks

Cheque de viajero

CHⓔ́-Kⓔ̃S Dⓔ VⒺⒺ-ⓐ-Hⓔ́-Rⓞ

Currencies

Peso/Mexico	Euro/Spain	Sol/Perú
Pⓔ́-Sⓞ	ⓞⓞ́-Rⓞ	SⓞL
Balboa/Panamá	Colón/El Salvador	Peso/Chile
Bⓐ̃L-Bⓞ́-ⓐ	Kⓞ-Lⓞ́N	Pⓔ́-Sⓞ

USEFUL PHRASES

Where is the bank?

¿Dónde está el banco?

DON-De eS-Tah eL BahN-KO

What time does the bank open?

¿A qué hora abre el banco?

ah Ke O-Rah ah-BRe

eL BahN-KO

Where is the exchange office?

¿Dónde está la casa de cambio?

DON-De eS-Tah Lah Kah-Sah

De KahM-Bee-O

What time does the exchange office open?

¿A qué hora abre la casa de cambio?

ah Ke O-Rah ah-BRe Lah

Kah-Sah De KahM-Bee-O

Can I change dollars here?

¿Puedo cambiar dólares aquí?

PWe-DO KahM-Bee-ahR

DO-Lah-ReS ah-KEE

Can you change this?

¿Me puede cambiar esto?

Mĕ PWĕ-Dĕ KⓐhM-BⓔⒺ-ⓐhR ĕ́S-Tⓞ

What is the exchange rate?

¿A cuánto está el cambio?

ⓐh KWⓐhN-Tⓞ ĕS-Tⓐh́ ĕL KⓐhM-BⓔⒺ-ⓞ

I would like large bills.

Quisiera billetes grandes.

KⒺⒺ-SⒺⒺ-ĕ́-Rⓐh BⓔⒺ-Yĕ́-Tĕs GRⓐhN-Dĕs

I would like small bills.

Quisiera billetes pequeños.

KⒺⒺ-SⒺⒺ-ĕ́-Rⓐh BⓔⒺ-Yĕ́-Tĕs Pĕ-Kĕ́N-Yⓞs

I need change.

Necesito cambio.

Nĕ-Sĕ-SⒺⒺ́-Tⓞ KⓐhM-BⓔⒺ-ⓞ

Do you have an ATM?

¿Tienen cajero automático?

TⒺⒺ-ĕ-Nĕ́N Kⓐh-Hĕ́R-ⓞ ⓞW-Tⓞ-Mⓐh́-TⒺⒺ-Kⓞ

POST OFFICE

If you are planning to send letters and postcards, be sure to send them early so that you don't arrive home before they do. **Correo** identifies the post office.

KEY WORDS

Airmail

Por avión

POR ah-VEE-ON

Letter

La carta

Lah KahR-Tah

Post office

El correo

EL KO-BE-O

Postcard

La tarjeta postal

Lah TahR-HE-Tah POS-TahL

Stamp

El sello

EL SE-YO

USEFUL PHRASES

Where is the post office?

¿Dónde está el correo?

DÓN-Dℯ ℯS-Tah ℯL KO-Rℯ-O

What time does the post office open?

¿A qué hora abren los correos?

ah Kℯ Ó-Rah ahB-RℯN
LOS KO-Rℯ-OS

I need stamps.

Necesito unos sellos.

Nℯ-Sℯ-SEE-TO oo-NOS Sℯ-YOS

I need an envelope.

Necesito un sobre.

Nℯ-Sℯ-SEE-TO ooN SÓ-BRℯ

I need a pen.

Necesito una pluma.

Nℯ-Sℯ-SEE-TO oo-Nah PLoo-Mah

TELEPHONE

Placing phone calls in a foreign country can be a test of will and stamina! Besides the obvious language barriers, service can vary greatly from one town to the next.

• If you have a choice, do not call from your hotel room. Service charges can add a hefty amount to your bill. If you use your hotel for long distance or international calls, use a Calling Card. This will cost you less than hotel charges; however, a fee may still be charged.

• In Spain, try to get to the CENTRAL TELEFONICA (CTNE). Here you can get assistance placing your call. You pay as soon as the call is completed.

• Calls can be made at telephone call centers and paid afterwards. There are also telephones in bars which cost more to use.

• In Mexico, you can purchase calling cards in stores, supermarkets, and newsstands. They can be used in "yellow" Telmex/Ladatel phone booths.

KEY WORDS

Information

Información

ⒺN-FⓄR-Mⓐⓗ-SⒺⒺ-ⓄʼN

Long distance

Larga distancia

LⓐⓗʼR-Gⓐⓗ DⒺⒺS-TⓐⓗʼN-SⒺⒺ-ⓐⓗ

Operator

La operadora

Lⓐⓗ Ⓞ-Pⓔ̆-Rⓐⓗ-DⓄʼR-ⓐⓗ

Phone book

La guía telefónica

Lⓐⓗ GⒺⒺʼ-ⓐⓗ Tⓔ̆-Lⓔ̆-FⓄʼ-NⒺⒺ-Kⓐⓗ

Public telephone

Teléfono público

Tⓔ̆-Lⓔ̆-FⓄ-NⓄ PⓞⓞʼB-LⒺⒺ-KⓄ

Telephone

El teléfono

ⓔ̆L Tⓔ̆-Lⓔ̆ʼ-FⓄ-NⓄ

USEFUL PHRASES

May I use your telephone?

¿Puedo usar su teléfono?

PWĒ-DO ͦͦ-Sah̃R S ͦͦ

TĒ-LĒ-FO-NO

Operator, I don't speak Spanish.

Operadora, no hablo español.

O-PĒ-Rah-DO′R-ah NO ah′B-LO

ĒS-Pah̃N-YO′L

I would like to make a long-distance call.

Quisiera hacer una llamada de larga
distancia.

KĒE-SĒE-Ē′-Rah ah-SĒ′R ͦͦ-Nah

Yah-Mah′-Dah DĒ Lah′R-Gah

DĒES-Tah̃NSĒE-ah

I would like to make a call to the United States.

Quisiera hacer una llamada a los Estados
Unidos.

KĒE-SĒE-Ē′-Rah ah-SĒ′R ͦͦ-Nah

Yah-Mah′-Dah ah LOS ĒS-Tah′-DOS

ͦͦ-NĒE′-DOS

I want to call this number...

Quiero llamar a este número...

KEE-ě-RO Yah-MahR ah ěS-Tě
NOO-Mě-RO...

SIGHTSEEING AND ENTERTAINMENT

In most cities and towns in Spanish-speaking countries, you will find tourist information offices. Here you can usually obtain brochures, maps, historical information, bus and train schedules.

CITIES IN MEXICO

Ciudad de México
SEE-oo-DahD DĕE MĕE-HEE-KO

Acapulco
ah-Kah-PooL-KO

Cancún
KahN-KooN

CITIES IN SOUTH AMERICA

Buenos Aires
BWĕE-NOS Ī-RĕES

Santiago
SahN-TEE-ah-GO

Bogotá
BO-GO-Tah

Lima
LEE-Mah

CITIES IN SPAIN

Madrid
Mah-DRĕED

Barcelona
BahR-THĕE-LO-Nah

Sevilla (Seville)
Sĕ-VEE-Yah

Pamplona
PahM-PLO-Nah

KEY WORDS

Admission

La admisión

L@h @hD-M@E-S@E-O'N

Map

El mapa

@L M@h'-P@h

Reservation

La reservación

L@h R@E-S@ER-V@h-S@E-O'N

Ticket

El boleto   El billete

@L B@O-L@E'-T@O   @L B@EE-Y@E'-T@E

Tour

La excursión

L@h @EKS-K@OR-S@E-O'N

Tour guide

El guía turístico

@L G@EE'-@h T@OO-R@EE'S-T@EE-K@O

USEFUL PHRASES

Where is the tourist office?

¿Dónde está la oficina de turismo?

DON-D℮ ℮S-Tah Lah
O-FEE-SEE-Nah D℮ TOO-REEZ-MO

Is there a tour to...?

¿Hay una excursión a...?

I OO-Nah ℮KS-KOOR-SEE-ON ah...

Where do I buy a ticket?

¿Dónde compro la entrada?

DON-D℮ KOM-PRO Lah
℮N-TRah-Dah

How much does the tour cost?

¿Cuánto cuesta la excursión?

KWahN-TO KW℮S-Tah Lah
℮KS-KOOR-SEE-ON

How long does the tour take?

¿Cuánto dura la excursión?

KWahN-TO DOO-Rah Lah
℮KS-KOOR-SEE-ON

Does the guide speak English?

¿Habla inglés el guía?

ⓐ́-BLⓐ ⒺN-GLⒺ́S ⒺL GⒺⒺ-ⓐ

Are children free?

¿Pagan los niños?

Pⓐ́-Gⓐ́N LⓄS NⒺⒺ́N-YⓄS

What time does the show start?

¿A qué hora empieza la función?

ⓐ KⒺ́ Ⓞ́-Rⓐ ⒺM-PⒺⒺ-Ⓔ́-Sⓐ
Lⓐ FⓄⓄN-SⒺⒺ-Ⓞ́N

Do I need reservation?

¿Necesito una reserva?

NⒺ́-SⒺ́-SⒺⒺ́-TⓄ ⓄⓄ́-Nⓐ
RⒺ́-SⒺ́R-Vⓐ

Where can we go dancing?

¿Dónde está la disco?

DⓄ́N-DⒺ́ Ⓔ́S-Tⓐ́ Lⓐ DⒺⒺ́S-KⓄ

Is there a minimum cover charge?

¿Hay un cargo mínimo?

Ⓘ ⓄⓄN Kⓐ́R-GⓄ MⒺⒺ́-NⒺⒺ-MⓄ

PHRASEMAKER

May I invite you…

¿Quisiera invitarla…

KⓔⒺ-SⓔⒺ-ⓔ́-Rⓐⓗ ⒺⒺN-VⓔⒺ-TⓐⓗR-Lⓐⓗ…

▸ **to a concert?**

a un concierto?

ⓐⓗ ⓄⓄN KⓄN-SⓔⒺ-ⓔ́R-TⓄ

▸ **to dance?**

a bailar?

ⓐⓗ BⓄⒾ-Lⓐⓗ́R

▸ **to dinner?**

a cenar?

ⓐⓗ Sⓔ̃-Nⓐⓗ́R

▸ **to the movies?**

al cine?

ⓐⓗL SⓔⒺ́-Nⓔ̃

▸ **to the theater?**

al teatro?

ⓐⓗL Tⓔ̃-ⓐⓗ́-TRⓄ

PHRASEMAKER

Where can I find…

¿Dónde se encuentra…

DⓄN-DⒺ SⒺ ⒺN-KWⒺN-TRⓐ…

▶ **a health club?**

un gimnasio?

ⓄN HⒺM-Nⓐ-SEE-Ⓞ

▶ **a swimming pool?**

una piscina?

Ⓞ-Nⓐ PEE-SEE-Nⓐ

▶ **a tennis court?**

una cancha de tenis?

Ⓞ-Nⓐ KⓐN-CHⓐ DⒺ TⒺ-NEES

▶ **a golf course?**

un campo de golf?

ⓄN KⓐM-PⓄ DⒺ GⓄLF

HEALTH

Hopefully you will not need
medical attention on your trip.
If you do, it is important to
communicate basic information regarding your condition.

- Check with your insurance
  company before leaving home to find out if
  you are covered in a foreign country. You may
  want to purchase traveler's insurance before
  leaving home.

- If you take prescription medicine, carry your
  prescription with you. Have your prescriptions
  translated before you leave home.

- Take a small first-aid kit with you.

- Your embassy or consulate should be able to
  assist you in finding health care.

- In Mexico, some pharmacies are open 24
  hours and others close around 10:00 PM.

- Some hotels can recommend English-speaking
  doctors and others have a doctor on call.

- In Spain, a **GREEN CROSS** indicates a
  pharmacy, where you can get basic medical
  information.

KEY WORDS

Ambulance

La ambulancia

L@h @hM-B@o-L@hN-S@-@h

Dentist

El dentista

@L D@N-T@S-T@h

Doctor

El médico

@L M@-D@-K@

Emergency

La emergencia

L@h @-M@R-H@N-S@-@h

Hospital

El hospital

@L @S-P@-T@hL

Prescription

La receta

L@h R@-S@-T@h

USEFUL PHRASES

I am sick.

Estoy enfermo. (male)

ⒺS-Tⓞⓨ́ ⒺN-FⒺ́Ʀ-MⓄ

I am sick.

Estoy enferma. (female)

ⒺS-Tⓞⓨ́ ⒺN-FⒺ́Ʀ-Mⓐⓗ

I need a doctor.

Necesito un médico.

NⒺ-SⒺ-SⒺ́-TⓄ ⓄⓄN MⒺ́-DⒺⒺ-KⓄ

It's an emergency!

¡Es una emergencia!

ⒺS ⓄⓄ́-Nⓐⓗ Ⓔ-MⒺⒷ-HⒺ́N-SⒺⒺ-ⓐⓗ

Where is the nearest hospital?

¿Dónde está el hospital más cercano?

DⓄ́N-DⒺ ⒺS-Tⓐⓗ́ ⒺL ⓄS-PⒺⒺ-Tⓐⓗ́L
Mⓐⓗ́S SⒺⒷ-Kⓐⓗ́-NⓄ

Call an ambulance!

¡Llame una ambulancia!

Yⓐⓗ́-MⒺ ⓄⓄ́-Nⓐⓗ ⓐⓗM-BⓄⓄ-Lⓐⓗ́N-SⒺⒺ-ⓐⓗ

I'm allergic to…

Tengo alergias a…

TⓔN-GⓄ ⓐⓗ-LⓔR-HⒺⒺ-ⓐⓗS ⓐⓗ…

I'm pregnant.

Estoy embarazada.

ⓔS-Tⓞⓨ ⓔM-Bⓐⓗ-Rⓐⓗ-Sⓐⓗ-Dⓐⓗ

I'm diabetic.

Soy diabético. (male)

Sⓞⓨ DⒺⒺ-ⓐⓗ-Bⓔ-TⒺⒺ-KⓄ

I'm diabetic.

Soy diabética. (female)

Sⓞⓨ DⒺⒺ-ⓐⓗ-Bⓔ-TⒺⒺ-Kⓐⓗ

I have a heart condition.

Sufro del corazón.

SⓄⓄ-FRⓄ DⓔL KⓄ-Rⓐⓗ-SⓄN

I have high blood pressure.

Tengo la presión alta.

TⓔN-GⓄ Lⓐⓗ PRⓔ-SⒺⒺ-ⓄN ⓐⓗL-Tⓐⓗ

I have low blood pressure.

Tengo la presión baja.

TⓔN-GⓄ Lⓐⓗ PRⓔ-SⒺⒺ-ⓄN Bⓐⓗ-Hⓐⓗ

PHRASEMAKER

I need…

Necesito…

Nĕ-Sĕ-SĒ´-TⓄ…

▸ **a doctor**

un médico

ⓄN MĔ´-DⒺⒺ-KⓄ

▸ **a dentist**

un dentista

ⓄN DĔN-TⒺⒺ´S-Tⓐ

▸ **a nurse**

una enfermera

ⓄⓄ´-Nⓐ ĔN-FĔR-MĔ´-Rⓐ

▸ **an optician**

un optometrista

ⓄN ⓄP-TⓄ-MĔ-TⓇⒺⒺ´S-Tⓐ

▸ **a pharmacist**

un farmacéutico

ⓄN Fⓐ R-Mⓐ-SⓄⓄ´-TⒺⒺ-KⓄ

PHRASEMAKER
(AT THE PHARMACY)

Do you have…

¿Tiene usted…

TEE-ê-Nê ⓞⓞS-TêD…

▸ **aspirin?**

aspirinas?

ⓐⓗS-PEE-REE-NⓐⓗS

▸ **Band-Aids?**

curitas?

Kⓞⓞ-REE-TⓐⓗS

▸ **cough syrup?**

calmante de la tos?

KⓐⓗL-MⓐⓗN-Tê Dê Lⓐⓗ TⓄS

▸ **ear drops?**

gotas para los oídos?

GⓄ-TⓐⓗS Pⓐⓗ-Rⓐⓗ LⓄS Ⓞ-EE-DⓄS

▸ **eyedrops?**

gotas para los ojos?

GⓄ-TⓐⓗS Pⓐⓗ-Rⓐⓗ LⓄS Ⓞ-HⓄS

BUSINESS TRAVEL

It is important to show appreciation and interest in another person's language and culture, particularly when doing business. A few well-pronounced phrases can make a great impression.

I have an appointment.

Tengo una cita.

TĔN-GŌ ōō-Nah SĔĔ-Tah

Here is my card.

Aquí tiene mi tarjeta personal.

ah-KĔĔ TĔĔ-ĕ-NĔ MĔĔ
Tah-R-Hĕ-Tah PĔR-SŌ-Nah'L

Can we get an interpreter?

¿Hay un intérprete?

Ī ōōN ĔĔN-TĔR-PRĔ-Tĕ

May I speak to Mr...?

¿Se encuentra el señor...?

SĔ ĔN-KWĔN-TRah ĔL SĔN-YŌR...

May I speak to Mrs...?

¿Se encuentra la señora...?

SĔ ĔN-KWĔN-TRah Lah SĔN-YŌ-Rah...

KEY WORDS

Appointment

La cita

L@h S@E-T@h

Mr.

El señor

@L S@N-Y@B

Mrs.

La señora

L@h S@N-Y@-B@h

Meeting

La reunión

L@h B@-@N-Y@N

Marketing

El mercado técnico

@L M@B-K@h-D@ T@K-N@E-K@

Presentation

La presentación

L@h PB@-S@N-T@h-S@E-@N

Sales

Las ventas

L@hS V@N-T@hS

PHRASEMAKER

I need…

Necesito…

Nẽ-Sẽ-SẼẼ-TO…

▶ **a computer**

una computadora
un ordenador (Spain)

OO-Nah KOM-POO-Tah-DO-Rah

ON OR-Dẽ-Nah-DOR

▶ **a copy machine**

una máquina para hacer copias

OO-Nah Mah-KEE-Nah Pah-Rah

ah-SẼR KO-PEE-ahS

▶ **a conference room**

un salón de conferencias

ON Sah-LON Dẽ KON-Fẽ-Rẽ̃N-SEE-ahS

▶ **a fax machine**

un fax

ON FahKS

▶ **an interpreter**

un intérprete

ON EEN-TẽR-PRẽ-Tẽ

▶ **a lawyer**

un abogado

OON ah-BO-Gah-DO

▶ **a notary**

un notario

OON NO-Tah-REE-O

▶ **overnight delivery**

entrega expresa
entrega inmediata (Spain)

eN-TReē-Gah eKS-PReē-Sah

eN-TReē-Gah EEN-Meē-Dee-ah-Tah

▶ **paper**

papel

Pah-PeēL

▶ **pen**   ▶ **pencil**

pluma   lápiz

PLoo-Mah   Lah-PEEZ

▶ **a secretary**

una secretaria

oo-Nah Seē-KReē-Tah-REE-ah

GENERAL INFORMATION

Climate in Latin America and Spain is diverse. Weather is largely affected by altitude and terrain.

SEASONS

Spring

La primavera

L@h PR@@-M@h-V@́-R@h

Summer

El verano

@L V@́-R@h-N@

Autumn

El otoño

@L @-T@́N-Y@

Winter

El invierno

@L @@N-V@@-@́R-N@

THE DAYS

Monday
lunes
LOO-NĕS

Tuesday
martes
Mah'R-TĕS

Wednesday
miércoles
MĒE-ĕ'R-KO-LĕS

Thursday
jueves
WHĕ'-VĕS

Friday
viernes
VĒE-ĕ'R-NĕS

Saturday
sábado
Sah'-Bah-DO

Sunday
domingo
DO-MĒEN-GO

THE MONTHS

January
enero
Ⓔ-NⒺ-ⓇⓄ

February
febrero
FⒺ-BRⒺ-ⓇⓄ

March
marzo
MⒶⒽB-SⓄ

April
abril
ⒶⒽ-BRⒺL

May
mayo
MⒶⒽ-YⓄ

June
junio
HⓄⓄ-NⒺⒺ-Ⓞ

July
julio
HⓄⓄ-LⒺⒺ-Ⓞ

August
agosto
ⒶⒽ-GⓄS-TⓄ

September
septiembre
SⒺP-TⒺⒺ-ⒺM-BRⒺ

October
octubre
ⓄK-TⓄⓄ-BRⒺ

November
noviembre
NⓄ-VⒺⒺ-ⒺM-BRⒺ

December
diciembre
DⒺⒺ-SⒺⒺ-ⒺM-BRⒺ

COLORS

Black	**White**
Negro	Blanco
NĒ-GRO	BLahN-KO
Blue	**Brown**
Azul	Café
ah-SOOL	Kah-FĒ
Gray	**Gold**
Gris	Oro
GREES	O-RO
Orange	**Yellow**
Anaranjado	Amarillo
ah-Nah-Rah-Hah-DO	ah-Mah-REE-YO
Red	**Green**
Rojo	Verde
RO-HO	VĒR-DĒ
Pink	**Purple**
Rosado	Morado
RO-Sah-DO	MO-Rah-DO

NUMBERS

0	**1**	**2**
Cero	Uno	Dos
Sĕ́-R⦿	ⓞⓞ́-N⦿	D⦿S

3	**4**	**5**
Tres	Cuatro	Cinco
TRĕ́S	KWah́-TR⦿	SḖN-K⦿

6	**7**	**8**
Seis	Siete	Ocho
S④S	SḖ-ĕ́-Tĕ	⦿́-CH⦿

9	**10**	**11**
Nueve	Diez	Once
NWĕ́-Vĕ	DḖ-ĕ́S	⦿́N-Sĕ

12	**13**	**14**
Doce	Trece	Catorce
D⦿́-Sĕ	TRĕ́-Sĕ	Kah́-T⦿́R-Sĕ

15	**16**	
Quince	Dieciséis	
KḖN-Sĕ	DḖ-ĕ́S-Ē-S④́S	

17

Diecisiete

DḖ-ĕ́S-Ē-SḖ-ĕ́-Tĕ

18

Dieciocho

DEE-eS-EE-O-CHO

19	**20**
Diecinueve	Veinte
DEE-eS-EE-NWe-Ve	VAN-Te

30	**40**
Treinta	Cuarenta
TRAN-Tah	KWah-ReN-Tah

50	**60**
Cincuenta	Sesenta
SEEN-KWeN-Tah	Se-SeN-Tah

70	**80**
Setenta	Ochenta
Se-TeN-Tah	O-CHeN-Tah

90	**100**
Noventa	Cien
NO-VeN-Tah	SEE-eN

1000	**1,000,000**
Mil	Millón
MEEL	MEE-YON

SPANISH VERBS

Verbs are the action words of any language. In Spanish there are three main types; **–ar**, **–er**, and **–ir**.

The foundation form for all verbs is called the infinitive. This is the form you will find in dictionaries. In English, we place "to" in front of the verb name to give us the infinitive; e.g., to speak. In Spanish. the infinitive is one word; **hablar**, and means by itself to speak, and (as in English) it does not change its form.

On the following pages you will see the present tense conjugation of the three regular verb groups: **–ar**, **–er**, and **–ir**. Conjugating a verb is what you do naturally in your own language: *I speak, he eats, they live*. A verb is called regular when it follows one of these three models: its basic form does not change, just the endings that correspond to the subject of the verb.

In your study of Spanish, you will come across irregular verbs and verbs with spelling changes. Their conjugation will require memorization. However, the Phrasemaker on page 128 will help you avoid this problem. First choose a form of want, then select an infinitive; 150 are provided in the following section. And because the infintive does not change, you don't need to worry about the conjugation of the verb or whether it is regular or irregular!

–AR VERB CONJUGATION

Find below the present tense conjugation for the regular **–AR** verb **hablar**, meaning **to speak**. The English equivalent is: *I speak* (or *I am speaking*), *you speak* (*you are speaking*), etc. For regular **–AR** verbs like this, drop the infinitive ending and add **-o**, **-as**, **-a**, **-amos**, **-áis** or **-an**.

I speak.

Yo hablo.

YO (ah)B-LO

You speak. (informal)

Tu hablas.

TOO (ah)B-L(ah)S

He speaks. / She speaks. / You speak. (formal)

El / Ella / Usted habla.

(e)L / (e)-Y(ah) / OOS-T(e)D (ah)B-L(ah)

We speak.

Nosotros hablamos.

NO-SO-TROS (ah)B-L(ah)-MOS

You speak. (plural)

Vosotros habláis.

VO-SO-TROS (ah)B-L(i)S

They speak.

Ellos / Ellas / Ustedes hablan.

(e)-YOS / (e)-Y(ah)S / OOS-T(e)-D(e)S (ah)B-L(ah)N

–ER VERB CONJUGATION

Find below the present tense conjugation for the regular
–ER verb **comer** meaning, **to eat**. The English equivalent
is: *I eat* (or *am eating*), *you eat* (*you are eating*), etc. For
regular **–ER** verbs like this, drop the infinitive ending
and add **-o**, **-es**, **-e**, **-emos**, **-éis** or **-an**.

I eat.

Yo com**o**.

YO̅ KO̅-MO̅

You eat. (informal)

Tu com**es**.

TŌŌ KO̅-MĒS

He eats. / She eats. / You eat. (formal)

El / Ella / Usted com**e**.

ĒL / Ē-Yah / ŌŌS-TĒD KO̅-MĒ

We eat.

Nosotros com**emos**.

NO̅-SO̅-TRO̅S KO̅-MĒ-MO̅S

You eat. (plural)

Vosotros com**éis**.

VO̅-SO̅-TRO̅S KO̅-MÁS

They eat.

Ellos / Ellas / Ustedes com**an**.

Ē-YO̅S / Ē-Yahs / ŌŌS-TĒD-ĒS KO̅-MĒN

–IR VERB CONJUGATION

Find below the present tense conjugation for the regular
–IR verb **vivir** meaning **to live**. The English equivalent
is: *I live* (or *I am living*), *you live* (*you are living*), etc.
For regular **–IR** verbs like this, drop the infinitive ending
and add **-o**, **-es**, **-e**, **-imos**, **-ís** or **-en**.

I live.

Yo viv**o**.

YO͞ V🄴🄴́-VO͞

You live. (informal)

Tu viv**es**.

TO͝O͝ V🄴🄴́-V🄴S

He lives. / She lives. / You live. (formal)

El / Ella / Usted viv**e**.

🄴L / 🄴́-Yah / O͝O͝S-T🄴D V🄴🄴́-V🄴

We live.

Nosotros viv**imos**.

NO͞-SÓ͞-TRO͞S V🄴🄴́-V🄴🄴́-MO͞S

You live (plural)

Vosotros viv**ís**.

VO͞-SÓ͞-TRO͞S V🄴🄴́-V🄴🄴S

They live.

Ellos / Ellas / Ustedes viv**en**.

🄴́-YO͞S / 🄴́-Yah S / O͝O͝S-T🄴́-D🄴S V🄴🄴́-V🄴N

PHRASEMAKER

I want...

Yo quiero...

YO KEE-ĕ-RO...

You want...

Tú quieres... (informal)

TOO KEE-ĕ-RĕS...

Usted quiere... (formal)

OOS-TĕD KEE-ĕ-Rĕ...

He wants... ◀

El quiere...

ĕL KEE-ĕ-Rĕ...

She wants... ◀

Ella quiere...

ĕ-Yah KEE-ĕ-Rĕ...

We want... ◀

Nosotros queremos..

NO-SO-TROS
KEE-ĕR-MOS...

They want...

Ellos quieren...

ĕ-YOS KEE-ĕ-RĕN...

It is easy to recognize Spanish verbs in their infinitive form because they always end in **-ar**, **-er**, or **-ir**!

▶ **to speak**

hablar

ahB-LahR

▶ **to eat**

comer

KO-MĕR

▶ **to live**

vivir

VEE-VĕR

150 VERBS

Here are some essential verbs that will carry you a long way towards learning Spanish with the EPLS Vowel Symbol System!

to add
añadir
@N-Y@-D̄EE̱R

to allow
permitir
P̄EE̱R-MEE̱-TEE̱R

to answer
responder
R̄EE̱S-P̄O̱N-D̄EE̱R

to arrive
llegar
YEE̱-G@R

to ask
preguntar
P̄R̄EE̱-G@N-T@R

to attack
atacar
@-T@-K@R

to attend
asistir
@-SEE̱S-TEE̱R

to bake (oven)
hornear
O̱R-NEE̱-@R

to be (temporary)
estar
EE̱S-T@R

to be (permanent)
ser
SEE̱R

to be able
poder
P̄O-D̄EE̱R

to beg
mendigar
MEE̱N-D̄EE̱-G@R

129

to begin

comenzar

KO-MEN-SahR

to believe

creer

KRE-ER

to break

romper

ROM-PER

to breathe

respirar

RES-PEE-RahR

to bring

llevar

YE-VahR

to build

construir

KON-STROO-EER

to burn

quemar

KE-MahR

to buy

comprar

KOM-PRahR

to call

llamar

Yah-MahR

to cancel

cancelar

KahN-SEL-ahR

to carry

llevar

YE-VahR

to change

cambiar

KahM-BEE-ahR

to chew

masticar

MahS-TEE-KahR

to clean

limpiar

LEEM-PEE-ahR

to climb
subir
Soo-BEER

to close
cerrar
Se-RahR

to come
venir
Ve-NEER

to cook
cocinar
KO-SEE-NahR

to count
contar
KON-TahR

to convert
convertir
KON-Ve-TEER

to cry
llorar
YO-RahR

to cut
cortar
KOR-TahR

to dance
bailar
BI-LahR

to decide
decidir
De-SEE-DEER

to depart
salir
Sah-LEER

to desire
desear
De-Se-ahR

disturb
molestar
MO-LeS-TahR

to do
hacer
ah-SeR

to drink

beber

Bē-Bēʳ

to drive

manejar

Mah-Nēē-Hahʳ

to dry

secar

Sē-Kahʳ

to earn

ganar

Gah-Nahʳ

to eat

comer

Kᴏ-Mēʳ

to explain

explicar

ēKS-PLēē-Kahʳ

to enjoy

disfrutar

DēēS-FRᴏᴏ-Tahʳ

to enter

entrar

ēN-TRahʳ

to feel

sentir

Sēn-Tēēʳ

to fight

luchar

Lᴏᴏ-CHahʳ

to fill

llenar

Yē-Nahʳ

to find

encontrar

ēN-Kᴏn-TRahʳ

to finish

terminar

Tēʳ-Mēē-Nahʳ

to fix

fijar

Fēē-Hahʳ

to fly volar VO-LahB	**to happen** pasar Pah-SahB
to follow seguir Se-GEeB	**to have** tener Te-NeB
to forgive perdonar PeB-DO-NahB	**to hear** escuchar eS-Koo-CHahB
to get obtener OB-Te-NeB	**to help** ayudar ah-Yoo-DahB
to give dar DahB	**to hide** ocultar O-KooL-TahB
to go ir EeB	**to hit** (fight) golpear GOL-Pee-ahB
to greet saludar Sah-Loo-DahB	**to imagine** imaginar Ee-Mah-HEe-NahB

to improve

mejorar

M@-HO-R@B

to judge

juzgar

H@S-G@B

to jump

saltar

S@L-T@B

to kiss

besar

B@-S@B

to know

saber

S@-B@B

to laugh

reír

R@-@B

to learn

aprender

@-PR@N-D@B

to leave

dejar

D@-H@B

to lie (not the truth)

mentir

M@N-T@B

to lift

levantar

L@-V@N-T@B

to like

gustar

G@S-T@B

to listen

escuchar

@S-K@-CH@B

to live

vivir

V@-V@B

to look

mirar

M@-R@B

to lose

perder

P⓮B-D⓮B

to love

amar

ⓐⱧ-MⓐⱧ'B

to make

hacer

ⓐⱧ-S⓮B

to measure

medir

M⓮-D⒠B

to miss

perder

P⓮B-D⓮B

to move

mover

Mⓞ-V⓮B

to need

necesitar

N⓮-S⓮-S⒠-TⓐⱧB

to offer

ofrecer

ⓞ-FB⓮-S⓮B

to open

abrir

ⓐⱧ-BB⒠B

to order

ordenar

ⓞB-D⓮-NⓐⱧB

to pack

empacar

⓮M-PⓐⱧ-KⓐⱧB

to pass (object/time)

pasar

PⓐⱧ-SⓐⱧB

to pay (for)

pagar

PⓐⱧ-GⓐⱧB

to play

jugar

Hⓞⓞ-GⓐⱧB

to pretend

pretender

PRē-TēN-DēR

to print

imprimir

ēM-PRēē-MēēR

to promise

prometer

PRō-Mē-TēR

to pronounce

pronunciar

PRō-NōōN-Sēē-ahR

to push

empujar

ēM-Pōō-HahR

to put

poner

Pō-NēR

to quit

dejar

Dē-HahR

to read

leer

Lē-ēR

to receive

recibir

Rē-Sēē-BēēR

to recomend

recomendar

Rē-Kō-MēN-DahR

to rent

alquilar

ahL-Kēē-LahR

remember

recordar

Rē-KōR-DahR

to rescue

rescatar

RēS-Kah-TahR

to rest

descansar

DēS-KahN-SahR

to return (an item)
volver
V(O)L-V(Ĕ)R

to run
correr
K(O)-R(Ĕ)R

to say
decir
D(Ĕ)-S(EE)R

to see
ver
V(Ĕ)R

to sell
vender
V(Ĕ)N-D(Ĕ)R

to show (display)
mostrar
M(O)S-TR(ah)R

to shower
duchar
D(oo)-CH(ah)R

to sign
firmar
F(EE)R-M(ah)R

to sing
cantar
K(ah)N-T(ah)R

to sit
sentar
S(Ĕ)N-T(ah)R

to sleep
dormir
D(O)R-M(EE)R

to smoke
fumar
F(oo)-M(ah)R

to smile
sonreír
S(O)N-R(A)-(EE)R

to speak
hablar
(ah)-BL(ah)R

to spell

deletrear

Dĕ-Lā-TRĕ-āR

to spend (time)

pasar

Pā-SāR

to start / to begin

empezar

ĕM-Pĕ-SāR

to stay

permanecer

PĕR-Mā-Nĕ-SĕR

to stop

parar

Pā-RāR

to study

estudiar

ĕS-Tō-Dē-āR

to succeed (achieve)

lograr

Lō-GRāR

to swim

nadar

Nā-DāR

to take

tomar

Tō-MāR

to talk

hablar

ā-BLāR

to teach

enseñar

ĕN-SĕN-YāR

to tell

decir

Dĕ-SēR

to touch (play instrument)

tocar

Tō-KāR

to think

pensar

PĕN-SāR

to travel
viajar
VEE-ah-HahR

to try (attempt)
tratar
TRah-TahR

to understand
comprender
KOM-PREN-DER

to use
usar
oo-SahR

to visit
visitar
VEE-SEE-TahR

to wait
esperar
ES-PE-RahR

to walk
caminar
Kah-MEE-NahR

to want
querer
KE-RER

to wash
lavar
Lah-VahR

to watch (look)
ver
VER

to win
ganar
Gah-NahR

to work
trabajar
TRah-Bah-HahR

to worry
preocupar
PRE-O-Koo-PahR

to write
escribir
ES-KREE-BER

DICTIONARY

Each English entry is followed by the Spanish word and the EPLS transliteration. Gender of nouns is indicated by (m) for masculine and (f) for feminine.

Plural is indicated by (/pl). Adjectives are shown in their masculine form, as common practice dictates. Adjectives and some nouns that end in **o** or **os** can usually be changed to feminine by changing the ending to **a** or **as**. Verbs appear in infinitive form, indicated by (to).

A

a, an un (m) / una (f) ⓞⓞN / ⓞⓞ-Nⓐⓗ

a lot mucho Mⓞⓞ-CHⓞ

able (to be) poder Pⓞ-THⓔⓡ

above sobre Sⓞ-BRⓔ

accident accidente (m) ⓐⓗK-Sⓔⓔ-Dⓔ́N-Tⓔ

accommodation alojamiento (m)
    ⓐⓗ-Lⓞ-Hⓐⓗ-Mⓔⓔ-ⓔ́N-Tⓞ

account cuenta (f) KWⓔ́N-Tⓐⓗ

address dirección (f) Dⓔⓔ-RⓔⓚⓚK-Sⓔⓔ-ⓞ́N

admission admisión (f) ⓐⓗD-Mⓔⓔ-Sⓔⓔ-ⓞ́N

afraid tener miedo Tⓔ́N-ⓔⓡ Mⓔⓔ-ⓔ́-THⓞ

after después DⓔⓢS-PWⓔ́S

---

afternoon tarde (f) TAHR-DE

air-conditioning aire acondicionado (m)
  I-RE ah-KON-DEE-SEE-O-Nah-DO

aircraft avión (m) ah-VEE-ON

airline línea aérea (f) LEE-NE-ah ah-E-RE-ah

airport aeropuerto (m) ah-E-RO-PWER-TO

aisle pasillo (m) Pah-SEE-YO

all todo TO-THO

almost casi Kah-SEE

alone solo SO-LO

also también TahM-BEE-EN

always siempre SEE-EM-PRE

ambulance ambulancia (f) ahM-BOO-Lah-N-SEE-ah

American americano (m) ah-ME-REE-Kah-NO
  americana (f) ah-ME-REE-Kah-Nah

and y EE

another otro O-TRO

anything algo ahL-GO

apartment apartamento (m) ah-Pah-Tah-MEN-TO

appetizers entremeses (m/pl) EN-TRE-ME-SES

apple manzana (f) MahN-Sah-Nah

appointment cita (f) SEE-Tah

April abril (m) ah-BREEL

arrival llegada (f) YEE-Gah-Dah

arrive (to) llegar YEE-Gahr

ashtray cenicero SEE-NEE-SEE-RO

aspirin aspirina (f) ah-SPEE-REE-Nah

attention ¡atención! ah-TEN-SEE-ON

August agosto (m) ah-GOS-TO

Australia Australia ow-STRA-LEE-uh

Australian Australiano (m) ow-STRA-LEE-uh-NO
Australiana (f) ow-STRA-LEE-uh-Nah

author autor (m) ow-TOR

automobile automóvil (m) ow-TO-MO-VEEL

autumn otoño (m) O-TON-YO

avenue avenida (f) ah-VEN-EE-Dah

awful horrible O-REE-BLE

B

baby bebé (m) BE-BE

babysitter niñera (f) NEEN-YE-Rah

bacon tocino (m) TO-SEE-NO

bad malo   MAH-LO

bag maleta (f)   MAH-LE-Tah

baggage equipaje (m)   E-KEE-PAH-HE

baked al horno   AHL OR-NO

bakery panadería (f)   PAH-NAH-DE-REE-ah

banana plátano (m)   PLAH-Tah-NO

Band-Aid curita (f)   KOO-REE-Tah

bank banco (m)   BAHN-KO

barbershop peluquería (f)   PE-LOO-KE-REE-ah

bartender cantinero (m)   KAHN-TEE-NE-RO

bath baño (m)   BAHN-YO

bathing suit traje de baño (m)
TRAH-HE DE BAHN-YO

bathroom baño (m)   BAHN-YO

battery batería (f) / pila (f)   BAH-TE-REE-ah / PEE-Lah

beach playa (f)   PLAH-Yah

beautiful bello   BE-YO

beauty shop salón de belleza (m)
SAH-LON DE BE-YE-Sah

bed cama (f)   KAH-Mah

beef carne de res (f)   KAHR-NE DE RES

beer cerveza (f)   SeR-Ve-Sah

bellman botones (m)   BO-TO-NeS

belt cinturón (m)   SeN-Too-RON

big grande   GRahN-De

bill cuenta (f)   KWeN-Tah

black negro   Ne-GRO

blanket cobija (f)   KO-Bee-Hah
    manta (f) (Spain)   MahN-Tah

blue azul   ah-Sool

boat barco (m)   BahR-KO

book libro (m)   Lee-BRO

bookstore librería (f)   Lee-BRe-Ree-ah

border frontera (f)   FRON-Te-Rah

boy muchacho (m)   Moo-CHah-CHO

bracelet pulsera (f)   Pool-Se-Rah

brake freno (m)   FRe-NO

bread pan (m)   PahN

breakfast desayuno (m)   De-Sah-Yoo-NO

broiled a la parrilla   ah   Lah   Pah-Ree-Yah

brown café   Kah-Fe

brush cepillo (m)   Se-Pee-YO

building edificio (m) ⓔ-Dⓔⓔ-Fⓔⓔ-Sⓔⓔ-Ⓞ

bus autobús (m) ⓪ⓦ-TⓄ-BⓞⓞˊS

bus station estación de autobuses (f)
ⓔ-STⓐⓗ-Sⓔⓔ-ⓄˊN Dⓔ ⓞⓦ-TⓄ-Bⓞⓞ-SⓔⓔS

bus stop parada de autobuses (f)
Pⓐⓗ-Rⓐⓗ-Dⓐⓗ Dⓔ ⓞⓦ-TⓄ-Bⓞⓞ-SⓔⓔS

business negocios (m) Nⓔⓔ-GⓄˊ-Sⓔⓔ-ⓄS

butter mantequilla (f) MⓐⓗN-Tⓔⓔ-Kⓔⓔˊ-Yⓐⓗ

buy (to) comprar KⓄM-PRⓐⓗR

C

cab taxi (m) TⓐⓗK-Sⓔⓔ

call (to) llamar Yⓐⓗ-MⓐⓗR

camera cámara (f) Kⓐⓗ-Mⓐⓗ-Rⓐⓗ

Canada Canadá Kⓐⓗ-Nⓐⓗ-Dⓐⓗˊ

Canadian el canadiense (m) ⓔL Kⓐⓗ-Nⓐⓗ-Dⓔⓔ-ⓔˊN-Sⓔ
(f) la canadiense Lⓐⓗ Kⓐⓗ-Nⓐⓗ-Dⓔⓔ-ⓔˊN-Sⓔ

candy dulce (m) DⓞⓞˊL-Sⓔ

car carro (m) / coche (m) / automóvil (m)
Kⓐⓗ-RⓄ / KⓄˊ-CHⓔ / ⓞⓦ-TⓄ-MⓄˊ-VⓔⓔL

carrot zanahoria (f) Sⓐⓗ-NⓄˊ-Rⓔⓔ-ⓐⓗ

castle castillo (m) Kⓐⓗ-STⓔⓔˊ-YⓄ

cathedral catedral (f) Kah-Tē-DRah'L

celebration celebración (f) Sē-Lē-BRah-Sē-O'N

center centro Sēn-TRO

cereal cereal (m) Sē-Rē-ē-ah'L

chair silla (f) Sēē-Yah

champagne champaña (m) CHahM-Pah'N-Yah

change (to) cambiar KahM-Bēē-ah'R

change (money) cambio (m) KahM-Bēē-O

cheap barato Bah-Rah'-TO

check (restaurant bill) cheque (m) CHē-Kē

cheers! ¡salud! Sah-Loo'D

cheese queso (m) Kē'-SO

chicken pollo (m) PO'-YO

child niño (m) / niña (f) Nēē'N-YO / Nēē'N-Yah

chocolate chocolate CHO-KO-Lah-Tē

church iglesia (f) ēē-GLē'-Sēē-ah

cigar puro (m) Poo'-RO

cigarette cigarrillo (m) Sēē-Gah-Rēē'-YO

city ciudad (f) Sēē-oo-Dah'D

clean limpio Lēē'M-Pēē-O

close (to) cerrar S@-B@B

closed cerrado S@-B@-DO

clothes ropa (f) BO-P@

cocktail cóctel (m) KOK-T@L

coffee café (m) K@-F@

cold (temperature) frío FB@-O

comb peine (m) P@-N@

come (to) venir V@-N@B

company compañía (f) KOM-P@N-Y@-@

computer computadora (f) KOM-P@-T@-DO-B@
ordenador (m) (Spain) OB-D@-N@-DOB

concert concierto (m) KON-S@-@B-TO

condom profiláctico (m) PBO-F@-L@K-T@-KO

conference conferencia (f) KON-F@-B@N-S@-@

conference room salón de conferencias (m)
S@-LON D@ KON-F@-B@N-S@-@S

congratulations felicitaciones (f/pl)
F@-L@-S@-T@-S@-O-N@S

copy machine máquina para hacer copias (f)
M@-K@-N@ P@-B@ @-S@B KO-P@-@S
Xerox (m) Z@-B@KS

corn maíz (m)   M@h-ẼS

cough syrup calmante de la tos (m)
K@hL-M@hN-Tẽ Dẽ L@h T◉S

cover charge cargo mínimo (m)
K@hB-G◉ MẼ-Nẽ-M◉

crab cangrejo (m)   K@hN-GBẽ-H◉

cream crema (f)   KBẽ-M@h

credit card tarjeta de crédito (f)
T@hB-Hẽ-T@h Dẽ KBẽ-Dẽ-T◉

cup taza (f)   T@h-S@h

customs aduana (f)   @h-DW@h-N@h

D

dance (to) bailar B◎-L@hB

dangerous peligroso Pẽ-Lẽ-GB◉-S◉

date (calendar) fecha (f)   Fẽ-CH@h

day día (m)   DẼ-@h

December diciembre (m)   DẼ-Sẽ-ẽM-BBẽ

delicious delicioso Dẽ-Lẽ-Sẽ-◉-S◉

delighted encantado ẽN-K@hN-T@h-D◉

dentist dentista (m)   DẽN-TẼS-T@h

deodorant desodorante (m)   Dẽ-S◉-D◉-B@hN-Tẽ

department store almacén (m) ahL-Mah-SeN

departure salida (f) Sah-LEE-Dah

dessert postre (m) POS-TRe

detour desviación (f) DeS-VEE-ah-SEE-ON

diabetic diabético (m) DEE-ah-BE-TEE-KO

diarrhea diarrea (f) DEE-ah-RE-ah

dictionary diccionario (m) DeK-SEE-O-Nah-REE-O

dinner cena (f) SE-Nah

dining room comedor (m) KO-Me-DOR

direction dirección (f) DEE-ReK-SEE-ON

dirty sucio SOO-SEE-O

disabled inválido (m) eN-Vah-LEE-DO

discount descuento (m) DeS-KWeN-TO
rebaja (f) Re-Bah-Hah

distance distancia (f) DeS-TahN-SEE-ah

doctor médico (m) ME-DEE-KO

document documento (m) DO-KOO-MeN-TO

dollar dólar (m) DO-LahR

down abajo ah-Bah-HO

downtown el centro eL SeN-TRO

dress vestido (m) VeS-TEE-DO

drink (to) beber Bⓔ-BⒺⓇ

drive (to) manejar Mⓐⓗ-Nⓔ-HⓐⓗⓇ

drugstore farmacia (f) FⓐⓗⓇ-Mⓐⓗ-SⒺⒺ-ⓐⓗ

dry cleaner tintorería (f) TⓔⒺN-TⓄ-Rⓔ-RⒺⒺ-ⓐⓗ

duck pato (m) Pⓐⓗ-TⓄ

E

ear oreja (f) / oído (m) ⓄⓇⒺ-Hⓐⓗ / Ⓞ-ⒺⒺ-THⓄ

ear drops gotas para los oídos (f/pl)
     GⓄ-TⓐⓗS Pⓐⓗ-Rⓐⓗ LⓄS Ⓞ-ⒺⒺ-DⓄS

early temprano TⓔⒺM-PRⓐⓗ-NⓄ

east este (m) ⓔⓗS-Tⓔ

easy fácil Fⓐⓗ-SⒺⒺL

eat (to) comer KⓄ-MⒺⓇ

egg huevo (m) Wⓔ-VⓄ

eggs (fried) huevos fritos (m/pl)
     Wⓔ-VⓄS FRⒺⒺ-TⓄS

eggs (scrambled) huevos revueltos (m/pl)
     Wⓔ-VⓄS Rⓔ-VWⓔL-TⓄS

electricity electricidad (f) ⓔ-LⓔK-TRⒺⒺ-SⒺⒺ-DⓐⓗD

elevator ascensor (m) ⓐⓗ-SⓔN-SⓄⓇ

embassy embajada (f) ⓔM-Bⓐⓗ-Hⓐⓗ-Dⓐⓗ

emergency emergencia (f) ĕ-MĔR-HĔN-SĔĔ-ah

England Inglaterra (f) ĔN-GLah-TĔ-Rah

English inglés (m) ĔN-GLĔS

enough! ¡Basta! Bah̃S-Tah

entrance entrada (f) ĕN-TRah-Dah

envelope sobre (m) SŌ-BRĕ

evening tarde (f) Tah̃R-Dĕ

everything todo TŌ-DŌ

excellent excelente ĕK-Sĕ-LĕN-Tĕ

excuse me perdón PĕR-DŌN

exit salida (f) Sah̃-LĔĔ-Dah

expensive caro Kah̃-RŌ

eye ojo (m) Ō-HŌ

eyedrops gotas para los ojos (f/pl)
GŌ-Tah̃S Pah̃-Rah LŌS Ō-HŌS

F

face cara (f) Kah̃-Rah

far lejos Lĕ-HŌS

fare billete (m) BĔĔ-Yĕ̃-Tĕ

fast rápido Rah̃-PĔĔ-DŌ

fax, fax machine fax (m) Fah̃KS

February febrero (m) FĒ-BRĒ-RO

few poco PŌ-KO

film (movie) película (f) PĒ-LĒ-KOO-Lah

film (camera) rollo de cámara (m)
　　RŌ-YO DĒ Kah-Mah-Bah

fine muy bien MWĒ BĒ-ĒN

finger dedo (m) DĒ-THO

fire fuego (m) FWĒ-GO

fire! ¡incendio! ĒN-SĒN-DĒ-O

fire extinguisher extintor (m) ĒKS-TĒN-TOB

first primero PRĒ-MĒ-RO

fish pescado (m) PĒS-Kah-DO

flight vuelo (m) VWĒ-LO

florist shop florería (f) FLO-BĒ-RĒ-ah

flower flor (f) FLOB

food comida (f) KO-MĒ-Dah

foot pie (m) PĒ-Ē

fork tenedor (m) TĒ-NĒ-DOB

french fries papas fritas (f/pl) Pah-Pah S FRĒ-Tah S
　　patatas fritas (Spain) Pah-Tah-Tah S FRĒ-Tah S

fresh fresco FRĒS-KO

Friday viernes (m)   VEE-ERR-NESS

fried frito   FREE-TO

friend amigo (m) / amiga (f)
   ah-MEE-GO / ah-MEE-Gah

fruit fruta (f)   FROO-Tah

funny gracioso   GRah-SEE-O-SO

G

gas station gasolinera (f)   Gah-SO-LEE-NEE-Rah

gasoline petróleo (m)   PE-TRO-LE-O

gate puerta (f)   PWERR-Tah

gentleman caballero (m)   Kah-Bah-YE-RO

gift regalo (m)   RE-Gah-LO

girl muchacha (f)   MOO-CHah-CHah

glass (drinking) vaso (m)   Vah-SO

glasses (eye) lentes (m/pl)   LEN-TESS

glove guante (m)   GWahN-TE

go vaya   Vah-Yah

gold oro (m)   O-RO

golf golf (m)   GOLF

golf course campo de golf (m)
   KahM-PO DE GOLF

good bueno BWⒺ-NⓄ

good-bye adiós ⓐ-DⒺⒺ-ⓄS

goose ganso (m) GⓐN-SⓄ

grapes uvas (f) ⓄⓄ-VⓐS

grateful agradecido ⓐ-GRⓐ-DⒺ-SⒺⒺ-DⓄ

gray gris GRⒺⒺS

green verde VⒺR-DⒺ

grocery store tienda de comestibles (f)
TⒺⒺ-ⒺN-Dⓐ DⒺ KⓄ-MⒺS-TⒺⒺ-BLⒺS

group grupo (m) GRⓄⓄ-PⓄ

guide guía (m) GⒺⒺ-ⓐ

H

hair cabello (m) Kⓐ-BⒺ-YⓄ

hairbrush cepillo (m) SⒺ-PⒺⒺ-YⓄ

haircut corte de pelo (m) KⓄR-TⒺ DⒺ PⒺ-LⓄ

ham jamón Hⓐ-MⓄN

hamburger hamburguesa (f) ⓐM-BⓄⓄR-GⒺ-Sⓐ

hand la mano (f) Lⓐ Mⓐ-NⓄ

happy feliz FⒺ-LⒺⒺS

have (to) tener TⒺN-ⒺR

he él ⓔL

head cabeza (f) Kⓐ-Bⓔ́-Sⓐ

headache dolor de cabeza (m)
Dⓞ-Lⓞ́B Dⓔ Cⓐ-Bⓔ́-Sⓐ

health club gimnasio (m) HⓔⓔM-Nⓐ́-Sⓔⓔ-ⓞ
club (m) KLⓞⓞB

heart corazón (m) Kⓞ-Bⓐ-Sⓞ́N

heart condition sufro del corazón (m)
Sⓞⓞ́-Bⓡⓞ Dⓔ́L Kⓞ-Bⓐ-Sⓞ́N

heat calefacción (f) Kⓐ-Lⓔ́-FⓐK-Sⓔⓔ-ⓞ́N

hello hola ⓞ́-Lⓐ

help! ¡socorro! Sⓞ-Kⓞ́-Bⓞ

here aquí ⓐ-Kⓔⓔ́

holiday día feriado (m) Dⓔⓔ́-ⓐ Fⓔ-Bⓔⓔ-ⓐ́-Dⓞ

hospital hospital (m) ⓞS-Pⓔⓔ-Tⓐ̀L

hot dog hot dog (m) Hⓐ̀T Dⓐ̀G

hotel hotel (m) ⓞ-Tⓔ̀L

hour hora (f) ⓞ́-Bⓐ

how ¿cómo? Kⓞ́-Mⓞ

hurry up! ¡apúrese! ⓐ-Pⓞⓞ́-Bⓔ́-Sⓔ̀

husband esposo ⓔS-Pⓞ́-Sⓞ

I

I yo   YŌ

ice hielo (m)   YĒ-LŌ

ice cream nieve (f)   NĒ-ē-Vē
helado (m) (Spain)   ē-Lāh-DŌ

ice cubes cubitos de hielo (m/pl)
KOO-BĒ-TŌS Dē YĒ-LŌ

ill enfermo   ēN-FēR-MŌ

important importante   ēM-PŌR-TāhN-Tē

indigestion indigestión (f)   ēN-DĒ-HēS-Tē-YŌN

information información (f)   ēN-FŌR-Māh-SĒ-ŌN

inn posada (f)   PŌ-Sāh-Dāh

interpreter intérprete (m)   ēN-TēR-PRē-Tē

J

jacket chaqueta (f)   CHāh-Kē-Tāh

jam mermelada (f)   MēR-Mē-Lāh-Dāh

January enero (m)   ē-Nē-RŌ

jewelry joyas (f)   HŌY-āhS

jewelry store joyería (f)   Hoy-e-REE-ah

job trabajo (m)   TRah-Bah-HO

juice jugo (m)   Hoo-GO

July julio (m)   Hoo-LEE-O

June junio (m)   Hoo-NEE-O

K

ketchup ketchup (m)   Ke-CHoo-P

key llave (f)   Yah-Ve

kiss beso (m)   Be-SO

knife cuchillo (m)   Koo-CHEE-YO

L

ladies' restroom servicios de señoras (m/pl)
    Se-VEE-See-OS De Se-N-YO-Rah-S

lady dama (f)   Dah-Mah

lamb cordero (m)   KOR-De-RO

language idioma (m)   EE-DEE-O-Mah

large grande   GRah-N-De

late tarde   Tah-R-De

laundry lavandería (f)   Lah-Vah-N-De-REE-ah

lawyer abogado (m)   ah-BO-Gah-DO

left (direction) izquierda ⓔS-Kⓔ-ⓔʳR-Dⓐh

leg pierna (f) Pⓔ-ⓔʳR-Nⓐh

lemon limón (m) Lⓔ-MⓄN

less menos Mⓔ-NⓄS

letter carta (f) KⓐʳR-Tⓐh

lettuce lechuga (f) Lⓔ-CHⓄⓄ-Gⓐh

light luz (f) LⓄⓄS

like (l) me gusta Mⓔ GⓄⓄS-Tⓐh

lip labio (m) Lⓐʰ-Bⓔⓔ-Ⓞ

lipstick pintura de labios (f)
     PⓔⓔN-TⓄⓄ-Rⓐh Dⓔ Lⓐʰ-Bⓔⓔ-ⓄS

little (amount) poquito PⓄ-Kⓔⓔ-TⓄ

little (size) pequeño Pⓔ-KⓔⓔN-YⓄ

live (to) vivir Vⓔⓔ-VⓔⓔʳR

lobster langosta (f) Lⓐ̃N-GⓄS-Tⓐh

long largo LⓐʳR-GⓄ

lost perdido PⓔʳR-Dⓔⓔ-DⓄ

love amor (m) ⓐʰ-MⓄʳR

luck suerte (f) SWⓔʳR-Tⓔ

luggage equipaje (m) ⓔ-Kⓔⓔ-Pⓐʰ-Hⓔ

lunch almuerzo (m) ⓐʰL-MWⓔʳR-SⓄ

M

maid camarera (f) Kah-Mah-Rê-Rah

mail correo (m) KO-Rê-O

makeup maquillaje (m) Mah-Kee-Yah-Hê

man hombre (m) OM-BRê

manager gerente (m) Hê-Rên-Tê

map mapa (m) Mah-Pah

March marzo (m) Mah-R-SO

market mercado (m) Mê-R-Kah-DO

match (light) cerillo (m), fósforo (m)
Sê-Rê-YO / FO-S-FO-RO

May mayo (m) Mah-YO

mayonnaise mayonesa (f) Mah-YO-Nê-Sah

meal comida (f) KO-Mê-Dah

meat carne (f) Kah-R-Nê

mechanic mecánico (m) Mê-Kah-Nê-KO

medicine medicina (f) Mê-Dê-Sê-Nah

meeting reunión (f) Rê-oo-Nê-ON

mens' restroom servicios de señores (m/pl)
Sê-R-Vê-Sê-OS Dê Sê-N-YO-Rê-S

menu menú (m) Mê-Noo

message recado (m)   Rĕ-K@-DO

milk leche (f)   Lĕ-CHĕ

mineral water agua mineral (m)
   @-GW@ Mēē-Nĕ-R@L

minute minuto (m)   Mēē-Noo-TO

Miss señorita (f)   SĕN-YO-Rēē-T@

mistake error (f)   ĕ-RŌR

misunderstanding equivocación (f)
   ĕ-Kēē-VO-K@-Sēē-ŌN

moment momento (m)   MO-Mĕ̈N-TO

Monday lunes (m)   Loo-NĕS

money dinero (m)   Dēē-Nĕ-RO

month mes (m)   MĕS

monument monumento (m)   MO-Noo-Mĕ̈N-TO

more más   M@S

morning mañana (f)   M@N-Y@-N@

mosque mezquita (f)   MĕS-Kēē-T@

mother madre (f)   M@-DRĕ

mountain montaña (f)   MON-T@N-Y@

movies cine (m)   Sēē-Nĕ

Mr. señor (m)   SĕN-YŌR

Mrs. señora (f)   SĕN-YŌ-R@

much (too) demasiado Dĕ-Mah-SEE-ah-DO

museum museo (m) Moo-SĕE-O

mushrooms hongos (m/pl) ON-GOS

music música (f) Moo-SEE-Kah

mustard mostaza (f) MOS-Tah-Sah

N

nail polish esmalte para uñas (m)
ĕS-Mah-L-Tĕ Pah-Rah oo-N-Yah-S

name nombre (m) NOM-BRĕ

napkin servilleta (f) SĕR-Vee-Yĕ-Tah

napkins (sanitary) almohadillas higiénicas (f)
ah-L-MO-Hah-Dee-Yah-S ee-Hee-ĕ-Nee-Kah-S

near cerca SĕR-Kah

neck cuello (m) KWĕ-YO

need (I) necesito Nĕ-Sĕ-SEE-TO

never nunca Noon-Kah

newspaper periódico (m) Pĕ-REE-O-Dĕ-KO

news stand quiosco de periódicos (m)
Kee-OS-KO Dĕ Pĕ-REE-O-Dĕ-KOS

night noche (f) NO-CHe

nightclub cabaret (m) Kah-Bah-ReT

no no NO

no smoking no fumar NO Foo-Mah'B

noon mediodía (m) Me-Dee-O-Dee-ah

north norte (m) NOB-Te

notary notario (m) NO-Tah-Ree-O

November noviembre (m) NO-Vee-eM-BRe

now ahora ah-O-Bah

number número (m) Noo-Me-BO

nurse enfermera (f) eN-FoB-Me-Bah

O

occupied ocupado O-Koo-Pah-DO

ocean océano O-Se-ah-NO

October octubre (m) OK-Too-BRe

officer oficial (m) O-Fee-See-ahL

oil aceite (m) ah-SA-Te

omelet tortilla de huevos (f)
    TOB-Te-Yah De We-VOS

one-way (traffic) una vía oo-Nah Vee-ah

onion cebolla (f) Se-BO-Yah

open (to) abrir ⓐ-ⒷⓇⒺⒷ

opera ópera (f) Ⓞ-Ⓟⓔ-Ⓡⓐ

operator operadora (f) Ⓞ-Ⓟⓔ-Ⓡⓐ-ⒹⓄⓇ-ⓐ

optician optometrista (m) ⓄⓅ-TⓄ-Mⓔ-TⓇⒺⓈ-Tⓐ

orange (color) anaranjado ⓐ-Nⓐ-ⓇⓐN-Hⓐ-ⒹⓄ

orange (fruit) naranja (f) Nⓐ-ⓇⓐN-Hⓐ

order (to) ordenar ⓄⓇ-Ⓓⓔ-NⓐⓇ

original original Ⓞ-Ⓡⓔ-Hⓔ-NⓐL

owner dueño (m) DWⓔN-YⓄ

oyster ostra (f) ⓄⓈ-TⓇⓐ

P

package paquete (m) Pⓐ-Kⓔ-Tⓔ

paid pagado Pⓐ-Gⓐ-ⒹⓄ

pain dolor (m) DⓄ-LⓄⓇ

painting pintura (f) PⒺN-Tⓞⓞ-Ⓡⓐ

pantyhose pantimedias (f/pl)
  PⓐN-TⒺ-Mⓔ-Dⓔ-ⓐⓈ

paper papel (m) Pⓐ-PⓔL

partner (business) socio (m) SⓄ-SⒺ-Ⓞ

party fiesta (f) FⒺ-ⓔⓈ-Tⓐ

passenger pasajero (m) Pah-Sah-Hē'-Ro

passport pasaporte (m) Pah-Sah-Po'R-Tē

pasta pasta (f) Pah'S-Tah

pastry pastel (m) Pah-STēL

pen pluma (f) PLoo-Mah

pencil lápiz (m) Lah'-Pēes

pepper pimienta (f) Pēe-Mēe-ē'N-Tah

perfume perfume (m) Pē'R-Foo-Mē

person persona (f) Pē'R-So'-Nah

person to person personal Pē'R-So-Nah'L

pharmacist farmacéutico (m) Fah'R-Mah-Soo-Tēe-Ko

pharmacy farmacia (f) Fah'R-Mah'-Sēe-ah

phone book guía telefónica (f)
   Gēe'-ah Tē-Lē-Fo'-Nēe-Kah

photo foto (f) Fo'-To

photographer fotógrafo (m) Fo-To'-GRah-Fo

pie pastel de (follow with name of filling)
   Pah-STēL Dē

pillow almohada (f) ahL-Mo-ah'-Dah

pink rosado Ro-Sah'-Do

pizza pizza (f) PEET-Sah or PEE-Sah

plastic plástico (m) PLahS-TEE-KO

plate plato (m) PLah-TO

please por favor POR Fah-VOR

pleasure placer (m) PLah-SeR

police policía (f) PO-LEE-SEE-ah

police station comisaría (f) KO-MEE-Sah-REE-ah

pork carne de puerco (f) KahR-NE DE PWeR-KO

porter maletero (m) Mah-LE-TE-RO

post office correo (m) KO-RE-O

postcard tarjeta postal (f) TahR-HE-Tah POS-TahL

potato papa (f) / patata (f) (Spain)
   Pah-Pah / Pah-Tah-Tah

pregnant embarazada eM-Bah-Rah-Sah-Dah

prescription receta (f) RE-SE-Tah

price precio (m) PRE-SEE-O

problem problema (m) PRO-BLE-Mah

profession profesión (f) PRO-FE-SEE-ON

public público PooB-LEE-KO

public telephone teléfono público (m)
   TE-LE-FO-NO PooB-LEE-KO

purified purificada   P☺☺-R☺☺-F☺☺-C☺☺-D☺☺

purple morado   M☺-R☺☺-D☺

purse bolsa (f)   B☺L-S☺☺

Q

quality calidad (f)   K☺☺-L☺☺-D☺☺D

question pregunta (f)   PR☺-G☺☺N-T☺☺

quickly rápido   R☺☺-P☺☺-D☺

quiet callado   K☺☺-Y☺☺-D☺

quiet! (be) ¡silencio!   S☺☺-L☺N-S☺☺-☺

R

radio radio (f)   R☺☺-D☺☺-☺

railroad ferrocarril (m)   F☺-R☺-K☺☺-R☺☺L

rain lluvia (f)   Y☺☺-V☺☺-☺☺

raincoat impermeable (m)
    ☺M-P☺R-M☺-☺☺-BL☺

ramp rampa (f)   R☺☺M-P☺☺

rare (cooked) poco cocida   P☺-K☺   K☺-S☺☺-D☺☺

razor blades hojas de afeitar (f/pl)
    ☺-H☺☺S   D☺   ☺☺-F☺-T☺☺R

ready listo (m) / lista (f)   L☺☺S-T☺ / L☺☺S-T☺☺

receipt recibo (m) Rē-SĒĒ-BO

recommend (to) recomendar Rē-KO-MĒN-DaⓗR

red rojo RŌ-HO

repeat! ¡repita! Rē-PĒĒ-Taⓗ

reservation reserva (f) / reservación (f)
Rē-SēR-Vaⓗ / Rē-SēR-Vaⓗ-SĒĒ-ŌN

restaurant restaurante (m) Rēs-Tow-Baⓗ-N-Tē

return devolver Dē-VOL-VēR

rice arroz (m) aⓗ-RŌS

rich rico RĒĒ-KO

right (correct) correcto KO-RēK-TO

right (direction) derecha Dē-Rē-CHaⓗ

road camino (m) Kaⓗ-MĒĒ-NO

room cuarto (m) KWaⓗR-TO

round trip ida y vuelta ĒĒ-Daⓗ ĒĒ VWēL-Taⓗ

S

safe (in a hotel) caja fuerte (f)
Kaⓗ-Haⓗ FWēR-Tē

salad ensalada (f) ēN-Saⓗ-Laⓗ-Daⓗ

sale venta (f) VēN-Taⓗ

salmon salmón (m) S@L-MÓN

salt sal (f) S@L

sandwich torta (f) TÓB-T@h
　　bocadillo (m) (Spain) BO-K@h-DEE-YO

Saturday sábado (m) S@h-B@h-DO

scissors tijeras (f/pl) TEE-HÉ-B@hS

sculpture escultura (f) ÉS-KOOL-TOÓ-B@h

seafood mariscos (m/pl) M@h-BEÉS-KOS

season estación (f) ÉS-T@h-SEE-ÓN

seat asiento (m) @h-SEE-ÉN-TO

secretary secretaria (f) S@-KB@-T@h-BEE-@h

section sección (f) S@K-SEE-ÓN

September septiembre (m) S@P-TEE-ÉM-BB@

service servicio (m) S@B-VEÉ-SEE-O

several varios V@h-BEE-OS

shampoo champú (m) CH@hM-Poo

sheets (bed) sábanas (f/pl) S@h-B@h-N@hS

shirt camisa (f) K@h-MEE-S@h

shoe zapato (m) S@h-P@h-TO

shoe store zapatería (f) S@h-P@h-T@-BEE-@h

shopping center centro comercial (m)
　　S@N-TBO KO-M@B-SEE-@hL

shower ducha (f)   DOO-CHah

shrimp camarones (m/pl)   Kah-Mah-BO-NeS

sick enfermo   eN-FeB-MO

sign (display) letrero (m)   Le-TBe-BO

signature firma (f)   FEEB-Mah

silence silencio   SEE-LeN-SEE-O

single solo   SO-LO

sir señor (m)   SeN-YOB

sister hermana (f)   eB-Mah-Nah

size tamaño (m)   Tah-MahN-YO

skin piel (f)   PEE-eL

skirt falda (f)   FahL-Dah

sleeve manga (f)   MahN-Gah

slowly despacio   De-SPah-SEE-O

small pequeño   Pe-KeN-YO

smoke (to) fumar   FOO-MahB

soap jabón (m)   Hah-BON

socks calcetas (f/pl) / calcetines (m/pl)
KahL-Se-TahS / KahL-Se-TEE-NeS

some unos (m/pl), unas (f/pl)   OO-NOS / OO-NahS
algunos / algunas (with numbers)
ahL-GOO-NOS / ahL-GOO-NahS

something algo @L-G©

sometimes algunas veces @L-G©©-N@S V©́-S©S

soon pronto PR©́N-T©

sorry (I am) lo siento L© S©-©́N-T©

soup sopa (f) / caldo (m) S©́-P@ / K@L-D©

south sur (m) S©©R

souvenir recuerdo (m) R©-KW©́R-D©

Spanish español (m) ©S-P@N-Y©́L

special especial ©-SP©-S©-@́L

speed velocidad (f) V©-L©-S©-D@́D

spoon cuchara (f) K©©-CH@́-R@

sport deporte (m) D©-P©́R-T©

spring (season) primavera (f) PR©-M@-V©́-R@

stairs escalera (f) ©S-K@-L©́-R@

stamp sello (m) / timbre (m) S©́-Y© / T©́M-BR©

station estación ©S-T@-S©-©́N

steak bistec (m) B©-ST©́K

steamed cocido a vapor K©-S©́-D© @ V@-P©́R

stop pare P@́-R©

store tienda (f) T©-©́N-D@

straight ahead derecho D©-R©́-CH©

strawberry fresa (f) FRĕ-Sah

street calle (f) Kah-Yĕ

string cuerda (f) KWĕR-Dah

subway metro (m) Mĕ-TRO
   subterráneo (m) (Spain) SooB-Tĕ-Rah-Nĕ-O

sugar azúcar (f) ah-Soo-KahR

suit (clothes) traje (m) TRah-Hĕ

suitcase maleta (f) Mah-Lĕ-Tah

summer verano (m) Vĕ-Rah-NO

sun sol (m) SOL

Sunday domingo (m) DO-MĕN-GO

sunglasses lentes de sol (f/pl) LĕN-TĕS Dĕ SOL

suntan lotion loción bronceadora (f)
   LO-Sĕĕ-ON BRON-Sĕ-ah-DOR-ah

supermarket supermercado (m)
   Soo-PĕR-MĕR-Kah-DO

surprise sorpresa (f) SOR-PRĕ-Sah

sweet dulce DooL-Sĕ

swim (to) nadar Nah-DahR

swimming pool piscina (f) Pĕĕ-Sĕĕ-Nah

synagogue sinagoga (f) SĕĕN-ah-GO-Gah

T

table mesa (f) MĒ-Sah

tampons tampones (m/pl) TahM-PŌ-NĒS

tape (sticky) cinta (f) SĒN-Tah

tape recorder grabador (m) GRah-Bah-DŌR

tax impuesto (m) ĒM-PWĒS-TŌ

taxi taxi (m) TahK-SĒ

tea té (m) TĒ

telegram telegrama (m) TĒ-LĒ-GRah-Mah

telephone teléfono (m) TĒ-LĒ-FŌ-NŌ

television televisión (f) TĒ-LĒ-VĒ-SĒ-ŌN

temperature temperatura (f) TĒM-PĒ-Bah-TŌŌ-Bah

temple templo (m) TĒM-PLŌ

tennis tenis (m) TĒ-NĒS

tennis court cancha de tenis (f)
   KahN-CHah DĒ TĒ-NĒS

thank you gracias GRah-SĒ-ahS

that ese (m) / esa (f) Ē-SĒ / Ē-Sah

the el (m) / la (f) / los (m/pl) / las (f/pl)
   ĒL / Lah / LŌS / LahS

theater teatro (m) TĒ-ah-TRŌ

there allí ah-YĒ

they ellos (m/pl) / ellas (f/pl) é-YOS / é-YahS

this este éS-Té

thread hilo (m) ÉE-LO

throat garganta (f) GahR-GahN-Tah

Thursday jueves (m) Hoo-é-VéS

ticket billete (m), boleto (m)
  BEE-Yé-Té / BO-Lé-TO

tie corbata (f) KOR-Bah-Tah

time tiempo (m) TEE-éM-PO

tip (gratuity) propina (f) PRO-PEE-Nah

tire llanta (f) YahN-Tah

tired cansado KahN-Sah-DO

toast pan tostado (m) PahN TO-STah-DO

tobacco tabaco (m) Tah-Bah-KO

today hoy OY

together juntos Hoo N-TOS

toilet baño (m) Bah N-YO

toilet paper papel higiénico (m)
  Pah-PéL EE-HEE-éN-EE-KO

tomato tomate (m) TO-Mah-Té
  jitomate (m) HEE-TO-Mah-Té

tomorrow mañana Mah N-Yah N-Nah

toothache dolor de dientes (m)
DO-LOB DE DEE-EN-TES

toothbrush cepillo de dientes (m)
SE-PEE-YO DE DEE-EN-TES

toothpaste pasta de dientes (f)
PAS-TA DE DEE-EN-TES

toothpick palillo (m) PA-LEE-YO

tour excursión (f) EKS-KOOB-SEE-ON

tourist turista (m) (f) TOO-BEES-TA

tourist office oficina de turismo (f)
O-FEE-SEE-NA DE TOO-BEEZ-MO

towel toalla (f) TO-A-YA

train tren (m) TBEN

travel agent agente de viajes (m)
A-HEN-TE DE VEE-A-HES

traveler's check cheque de viajero (m)
CHE-KE DE VEE-A-HE-BO

trip viaje (m) VEE-A-HE

trousers pantalones (m/pl) PAN-TA-LO-NES

trout trucha (f) TBOO-CHA

truth verdad (f) VEB-DAD

Tuesday martes (m) MAB-TES

U

umbrella paraguas (m) Pah-Rah-GWahS

understand (to) entender eN-TeN-DeR

underwear ropa interior (f) RO-Pah eN-Te-Ree-OR

United Kingdom Reino Unido (m)
RA-NO oo-Nee-DO

United States Estados Unidos (m/pl)
eS-Tah-DOS oo-Nee-DOS

university universidad (f) oo-Nee-VeR-See-DahD

up arriba ah-Ree-Bah

urgent urgente ooR-HeN-Te

V

vacant desocupado De-SO-Koo-Pah-DO

vacation vacaciones (f/pl) Vah-Kah-See-ON-eS

valuable precioso PRe-See-O-SO

value valor (m) Vah-LOR

vanilla vainilla (f) VI-Nee-Yah

veal carne de ternera (f)
KahR-Ne De TeR-Ne-Rah

vegetables legumbres (f/pl) / vegetales (m/pl)
Le-Goom-BReS / Ve-He-Tah-LeS

view vista (f) VeeS-Tah

vinegar vinagre (m) Vee-Nah-GRe

voyage viaje (m) Vee-ah-He

W

wait! ¡espérese! ⓔS-PⒺ-RⒺ-SⒺ

waiter camarero (m) Kⓐ-Mⓐ-RⒺ-RⓄ
  mozo (m) (Spain) MⓄ-THⓄ

waitress camarera (f) Kⓐ-Mⓐ-RⒺ-Rⓐ
  moza (f) (Spain) MⓄ-THⓐ

want (I) quiero KⒺ-Ⓔ-RⓄ

water agua (f) ⓐ-GWⓐ

we nosotros (m/pl) NⓄ-SⓄ-TRⓄS

weather tiempo (m) TⒺ-ⓔM-PⓄ

Wednesday miércoles (m) MⒺ-ⓔR-KⓄ-LⓔS

week semana (f) SⒺ-Mⓐ-Nⓐ

weekend fin de semana (m) FⒺN Dⓔ SⒺ-MⓐN-ⓐ

welcome ¡bienvenido! BⒺ-ⓔN-VⒺ-NⒺ-DⓄ

well cooked bien cocida BⒺ-ⓔN KⓄ-SⒺ-Dⓐ

west oeste (m) Ⓞ-ⓔS-TⒺ

what? ¿qué? KⒺ / ¿cómo? KⓄ-MⓄ

wheelchair silla de ruedas (f)
  SⒺ-Yⓐ Dⓔ Rⓞⓞ-Ⓔ-DⓐS

when? ¿cuándo? KWⓐN-DⓄ

where? ¿dónde? DⓄN-DⒺ

which? ¿cuál? KWⓐL

white blanco BL@N-K@

who? ¿quién? K@-@N

why? ¿por qué? P@B-K@

wife esposa (f) @S-P@-S@

window ventana (f) V@N-T@-N@

wine list lista de vinos (f) L@S-T@ D@ V@-N@S

wine vino (m) V@-N@

winter invierno (m) @N-V@-@B-N@

with con K@N

woman mujer (f) M@-H@B

wonderful maravilloso M@-B@-V@-Y@-S@

world mundo (m) M@N-D@

wrong equivocado / incorrecto
@-K@-V@-K@-TH@ / @N-K@-B@K-T@

XYZ

year año (m) @N-Y@

yellow amarillo @-M@-B@-Y@

yes sí S@

yesterday ayer @-Y@B

you usted (formal) @-ST@D / tú (informal) T@

zipper cierre (m) S@-@-B@

zoo zoológico (m) S@-@-L@-H@-K@

EASILY PRONOUNCED LANGUAGE SYSTEMS

Author Clyde Peters graduated from Radford High School and the University of Hawaii and has traveled the world as a travel writer. His innovative Say It Right phrase books have revolutionized the way languages are taught and learned. Mr. Peters invented the Vowel Symbol System for easy and correct pronunciation of virtually any language. He currently continues traveling the world working on new languages and divides his spare time between Las Vegas, Nevada, and Hawaii.

Betty Chapman is a successful business woman who along with Mr. Peters founded Easily Pronounced Language Systems to promote education, travel, and custom tailored language solutions. "Moving beyond expectation to acquisition and accomplishment is possible with EPLS."

Priscilla Leal Bailey is the senior series editor for all Say It Right products and has proved indispensable in editing and implementing the EPLS Vowel Symbol System. We are forever grateful for her belief and support.

SAY IT RIGHT SERIES
Infinite Destinations
One Pronunciation System!

Audio Editions

Say It Right App on iTunes

THANKS!

The nicest thing you can say to anyone in any language is "Thank you." Try some of these languages using the incredible EPLS Vowel Symbol System.

Arabic
SH⓪⓪-KRⓐⓗN

Chinese
SH㊙㊙⓪   SH㊙㊙ⓔ

French
MⓔⓇ-S㊙㊙

German
DⓐⓗN-KⓊⓗ

Hawaiian
Mⓐⓗ-Hⓐⓗ-L⓪

Italian
GRⓐⓗT-S㊙㊙-ⓔ

Japanese
D⓪-M⓪

Portuguese
⓪-BR㊙㊙-Gⓐⓗ-D⓪

Russian
SPⓐⓗ-S㊙㊙-Bⓐⓗ

Spanish
GRⓐⓗ-S㊙㊙-ⓐⓗS

Swahili
ⓐⓗ-SⓐⓗN-Tⓐ

Tagalog
Sⓐⓗ-Lⓐⓗ-MⓐⓗT